CU00647497

Michael Wachtler

The First World War in the Alps

English: Tom O'Toole

Right: A sentry with rifle stands guard on a precipice amid the majestic Ampezzo Dolomites. The photo has been coloured using the most modern technology.

First edition 2006

All rights reserved

Michael Wachtler
The First World War in the Alps

Publisher: Athesia Spectrum

English: Tom O'Toole

Produced by: Wachtler KG-Innichen

Printed by: Athesiadruck Bozen

ISBN 88-6011-037-8

e-mail: athesia.spectrum@athesia.it

e-mail: michael@wachtler.com

We would like to thank:
Tiroler Kaiserjäger Museum Berg Isel - Innsbruck, Paul Hoffmann, Museum 1915-18 Kötschach Mauthen, Walther Schaumann +
Günther Obwegs, Fabio Ortolani, Konrad Knoll, Paolo Giacomel, Marco Zardini
Museo della Grande Guerra, Val Parola, family Lancedelli
Museo della Guerra Bianca,Temù, John Ceruti and Walter Bellotti, Museo Storico di Trento,
Museo della Guerra Rovereto, Camillo Zadra,
Museo della Guerra, Peio, Maurizio Vincenzi

Michael Wachtler

The First World War in the Alps

Michael Wachtler

These makeshift wooden huts seem glued to the mountain on Monte Piano. Tyrolean territorial defenders carry firewood in the Ortler battle arena, though also furniture to a
position at an elevation of almost 4,000 metres (13,125 feet).

Contents

A life is extinguished. An Alpini soldier lies dead in the snow in the Lares ridge gap on the Adamello.

"The lamps are going out
all over Europe;
we shall not see them lit again
in our lifetime."
Sir Edward Grey 3rd August, 1914
British Foreign Minister

Of war in the mountains or the quest for peace

This war in the mountains of the eastern Alps was a war with a difference. Never before had men been expected to resist the elements at altitudes reaching almost 4,000 metres for months on end in bitter cold and snow. It is precisely for this reason that the war in this battlefield has taken a special place in history. It was an anachronistic struggle: the battles were still for the most part man against man, for no tank or other armoured vehicle could penetrate into these regions. Impartial nature entered the fray as a third, perhaps most terrible adversary. Avalanches swept thousands to their deaths, cold wore down men's spirits, lightning and thunder storms cowed the combatants.

Perhaps for this reason there were so many examples of comradeship and peace initiatives on these mountains, even if they only occurred between isolated groups and small numbers of men. And did not nature induce men to fraternise once again when a separate, secluded world came into being during the long winter months? When for months on end no news arrived from below and likewise no news reached the enemy? Very often individual soldiers, whether Italian or Austrians, all of the same social class, had no idea why they were fighting. So why should they not fraternise? In this spirit this book also tells of small and isolated attempts at making peace. There are many examples of a kind which today still move us to tears. There are the diaries of the eighteen-year-old Karl Mayr of the Standschützen (civil defence corps), or of the young Giacomo Perico, soldier in the Italian Alpine (Alpini) corps. All contributed to strengthening our faith in human goodness. The horrors of war appear even more brutal and senseless when described by men who took part. The racing heartbeat of a soldier who knows he will only survive this day by an extreme fluke of fortune, the wide-open eyes of a dying comrade, riddled by bullets, torn apart by shellfire. This book attempts to tell the story of the First World War in the Alps with the help of the most telling photos chosen from numerous archives. The events here contributed little to the Great War's outcome, though in their own way they were highly significant. Spectacular underground towns were created in the glacier ice with kilometre-long connecting corridors, entire mountaintops were blasted out of existence in attempts to dislodge just handfuls of opponents. This war set the course for winter tourism. Aerial cableways and lifts transported men and equipment into the high regions and skis became important means of locomotion in battle.

In the meantime these mountains have become enveloped in myth and legend. Still the struggle these men endured against the power of nature and the blind sway of dictatorial systems will remain unforgotten forever.

Michael Wachtler

Of war in the Alps

The landscape was so beautiful that it began to attract tourists in their thousands. Some were drawn by the desire to climb the peaks and become enshrined in the mountaineering hall of fame, while others were excited by the allure of adventure. Tectonic forces caused the earth's surface to upheave over millions of years to form the Alps, building a natural and formidable barrier in a region of the world where people of diverse language groups settled. Some peoples managed to form their own nations, the French, the Germans and Italians. And still linguistic groups found themselves as ethnic minorities inside larger territories. A case in point is the Austro-Hungarian monarchy. At the beginning of the 20th century the empire comprised a wild potpourri of peoples of the most diverse languages, religions and other cultural peculiarities. Italians, Ladins, Slavs, Croatians, Hungarians, Germans, Serbs, Czechs, Slovaks and plenty more besides were forced to get along with each other and in spite of enormous efforts and, for the times, astonish-

Günther Obwegs-Gottfried Letitgeb

"With God, for Emperor and the Fatherland – World War 1914-15" reads the inscription. Italy has just entered the war. The photo is of a motley crew of Standschützen, or civil defence militia. They believe they will be back home in time for the late summer hay harvest. A fateful illusion.

8

ingly tolerant government the undercurrents for future turmoil were gaining strength beneath the surface. Emperor Franz Joseph I had governed this multiracial commonwealth for decades. So long that most subjects had never known any other ruler.

However it is wrong to regard this odd entity as the precursor of a united Europe, as it is often praised by authors, in as much as it was basically a colonial empire under Austrian rule.

War came because it was inevitable and desired on the most diverse sides and for the most diverse reasons, and was supposed to less than a week, at the very most until Christmas 1914. It developed initially in the east, far away from these mountains, even if the hearts of these mountain people began to bleed as soon as the first war dead were brought home from Galicia.

A lonely war

At the outset Italy remained calm, even though there were plenty of signs that this increasingly powerful nation was thirsting to throw off centuries of humiliation. Finally in May 1915 a completely new kind of conflict was born: high altitude mountain war. It is true that Hannibal crossed the Alps 2,000 years earlier to attack the Romans from their rear, though nobody had previously imagined that men could wage war among these precipitous rock faces, in places at elevations exceeding 3,000 metres. In fact it was nobody's intention. Italy's strategy was to cross the passes quickly and then to advance at speed through the valleys to Vienna. However, events turned out differently.

It became a secluded, "lonely war" as the German military historian Heinz von Lichem described it, and the line extended from the Julian Alps in the east, across the Kärnten (Carinthian), Carnic Alps, the

Dolomites, Lake Garda to the Adamello and on to the Ortler as far as the Swiss border. It became a "front among rocks and ice", to use the words of war veteran Gunther Langes. At the time Austria and Italy shared an approximately three hundred and seventy kilometre border. This massif – comprising a large part of the Alps – formed a natural bulwark separating the Italian troops on the one side and the Austro-Hungarian army on the other. Nature quickly joined the combatants in these inhospitable regions as a third, and perhaps most terrible adversary.

A fatal hesitation on the part of Italy, perhaps brought about by the nation's overhasty entry into the war in May 1915,

Museum 1915-18 Kötschach-Mauthen

The soldiers' quarters on the Wischberg in the Julian Alps are situated beneath metres-high walls of snow.

9

meant that the strategy of overrunning the surprised and not yet organised Austrian troops was doomed to failure from the outset, the intention of breaching the defences on one of the many passes, whether the Plöcken and the Kanaltal valley, or the Kreuzberg Pass, or through the Höhlenstein Valley to enter the broad Pustertal

Italian Alpine troops (Alpini) bury one of their comrades. Wooden coffins were far from the norm, very often fallen soldiers were buried in mass graves.

valley, or to advance towards Vienna via Villach. For the so-called Freiwillige Schützen (volunteer homeland defence corps) in Kärnten, and the Tyrolean Standschützen (men aged over 45 and youths

under 18 - too old or too young for active service), were quickly deployed. Alpine born and bred, using their intimate knowledge of the local terrain, they began to occupy strategically important peaks and ridges. Though apart from their skills at shooting the Standschützen had hardly any military training. All of a sudden 50,000 defenders which nobody had reckoned with were available, 38,000 Standschützen and 12,000 Freiwillige Schützen. From then on villages in these areas were deprived of their menfolk, though for the most part women, children and the elderly quickly took over their tasks and cultivated the fields. They also ensured that men on the front were kept well-supplied with food and other provisions.

A series of salients and permanent fortifications, some antiquated, lined the entire frontier from the Stilfser Joch pass, Gomagoi, Riva, Lavarone, Tre Sassi, Landro, Sexten, Malborghet, Raibl and Predil with the purpose of warding off eventual Italian attacks. They had been built many years previously, obviously in anticipation that the 30-year-old treaty of friendship might not hold forever and that a war between the Austro-Hungarian empire and Italy could ensue. Italy was of course the hereditary enemy of the Habsburg monarchy and certainly no new opponent of the empire. Perhaps a heavier and more resolute Italian push across one of the lower passes or into one of the central valleys would still have resulted in the all-too-weak Austrian lines being penetrated. Such a tactic served the Austrians well later in autumn 1917 when they routed the demoralised Italian forces in the valley basin of Caporetto (called Karfreit by the Central Powers, now the village of Kobarid in Slovenia). Howev-

Museo Storico Trento

er the Italian commander-in-chief, General Luigi Cadorna advanced far too cautiously and slowly, - perhaps failed by his own intelligence service – and also through being disoriented by Austrian columns at the outset of the war. They marched and countermarched, constantly on the move between the Gailtal and Pustertal valleys with the sole purpose of misleading the Italians as to the strength of their forces. At least this feckless General Cadorna succeeded in one thing: tying up Austrian battalions for years which were desperately needed on other European fronts. Following the defeat on the Isonzo river he was eventually replaced on 8th November 1917 with General Armando Diaz in agreement with the Allies. Unlike Cadorna, who was just as much a political animal as he was a general, Diaz was more of a 'soldier's soldier', determined to pursue the war with tenacity and according to modern concepts rather than become involved with political intrigues in Rome.

With no sense of foreboding of what was to come, the combatants became bogged down in futile skirmishes for insignificant territorial gains. As the war progressed both sides became more and more entrenched in well-constructed and defended positions. The Italians were the assailants faced with the task of overrunning Austria. A heavy burden which inevitably led to the defeat of the Italian troops, an army randomly recruited from simple labourers and farmhands. However, it would be wrong to assert that Italian Alpini or Bersaglieri (light infantry) troops were weak adversaries. They made up for their lack of experience in mountain terrain partially through courage – after all, for the first time they were fighting for their own strong nation – and partially through the sheer numbers of men thrown into the

conflict as cannon fodder. Consequently casualties among Italian soldiers were far higher than those suffered on the Austrian side. Not counting the deaths caused by nature, through avalanches, rockfalls, by supplies being interrupted by severe weather, or other natural disasters. Nature claimed higher numbers of casualties than did the actual fighting in this 'Great War', as it still frequently called.

The Julian Alps

The main battleground in the Julian Alps was the Krn mountain, 2,245 metres high overlooking Caporetto, as the Italians christened the village of Kobarid in Slovenia once they had taken it (Karfreit in German). This summit soon became transformed into an impregnable and, for the times, highly mechanised fortress. The

Museum 1915-18 Kötschach-Mauthen

Italian and Austrian troops face each other in makeshift defences and fight fiercely on the Kleiner Pal. The picture shows an Italian position.

summit was of enormous strategic importance, for the entire Carinthian front could have collapsed had the Italians succeed in taking this position. Throughout the entire war the Austrians found keep-

A moment of relaxation for these Italian officers with their dogs. They are standing in front of their relatively comfortable huts. A privilege enjoyed by the few. Common soldiers did not even have a bed of their own. They slept wherever they could find room.

Massimo Turkheimer, Foto E.Turkheimer

ing open the lines of supply to be a far greater bane than being harassed by their Italian adversaries, above all when they were cut off for weeks on end due to the harsh winter weather. The Krn represented the cornerstone on the Isonzo front, the Rombon massif, almost equally high located near Flitsch, the other. The Italians actually managed to take the Rombon summit in August 1915 but were subsequently driven back. During the winter of 1916 it changed hands several times with heavy casualties and was only taken once and for all by the Carinthian defence troops following the breakthrough at Flitsch-Tolmezzo in October 1917. This hard struggle for every rock and stone encapsulated the entire action on the frontline and continued across the neighbouring mountain summits. Heroes were born equally on the Wischberg, the Montasch massif and the Grosser Nabois, all of them summits at altitudes between 2,500 and 2,700 metres above sea level, just as they were in

the Dolomites further west, the Adamello and the Ortler. Daring mountain climbers such as the engineer Ferdinand Horn undertook first ascents which few people deemed possible in order to penetrate behind the Italian positions and send back secret messages to their own troops using optical signals. Above all in the Montasch massif Austro-Hungarian troops attacked well-positioned Italian machine gun nests incurring high casualties.

The Italians had laboured for years to transform several mountain summits into invulnerable bastions which obstructed the route through the Isonzo Valley.

These summits are associated with the rise of a brilliant German strategist who was later to gain even greater renown in World War Two as the 'Desert Fox': First Lieutenant Erwin Rommel. He arrived in this area with the Württemberg Alpine battalion. In a surprise attack on 25th October 1917 he took the Kolovrat near Tolmein (Tolmezzo), a formidably constructed

Günther Obwegs/Gottfried Leitgeb

The Rederlechner family from Sand in Taufers in their parlour. Each had to do what they could to contribute to victory. Women mend worn-out war uniforms, the men enjoy their leave from the front.

summit fort which hermetically sealed off the area. The victory fed the young officer's ambition and appetite for action. A day later Monte Cragonza was captured. His fatigued men were allowed no respite. The next in line was Monte Matajur, a fortress with even stronger defences than all the others. This too fell to the German, completely unexpectedly and as an enormous surprise on both sides. Even then his assaults were based on independent, lightning-fast pincer movements followed by a swift retreat, his troops only to reappear at another position where the front was deemed weaker. Erwin Rommel received for his deeds the highest German military decoration, the Pour-le-Merite medal,– also known as 'The Blue Max' and his enterprises opened the way into the northern Italian plain. Twenty-five years later Rommel used the same tactics of speed and surprise as commander of the German Africa Corps in the desert and the Middle East. He became revered both for his military prowess and the chivalry he showed towards his adversaries. After a defeat at Rommel's hands the British Prime Minister Winston Churchill told the House of Commons: "We have a very daring and skillful opponent against us, and, may I say across the havoc of war, a great General".

In October 1917 Italy was to be dealt a fatal blow in the Julian Alps theatre, a success which Austria-Hungary hoped could be turned into a decisive victory. Paradoxically the crushing victory at Caporetto and breakthrough into the northern Italian plain sealed the fate of the Austro-Hungarian monarchy. In a very short time the frontier was reduced from 370 kilometres to a mere 130 and the Central Powers began talking reverently of the "wonder at Caporetto". However, the subject soon became the "wonder of Italy's resurrection". The demoralised Italian troops may have been lacking motivation while fighting a war of expansion, but now enemy forces

Austrian outposts on the fiercely contested Elfer in the Sexten Dolomites. Today these mountains are still remembered more for the mountaineering feats of individual soldiers than for large-scale combat.

had broken through onto their national territory. Venice, Verona, perhaps even Ravenna and Bologna were threatened. Under their new commander Diaz their spirits suddenly rallied. With allied support and a reinvigorated fighting spirit, soldiers began to protect the front and win back lost territory.

The Carnic Alps

The main ridge in the Carnic Alps runs from the Plöcken Pass near Kötschach-Mauthen to the Kreuzberg Pass. Mountains including the Grosse and Kleine Pall, the Rauchkofel, the Torkarspitze as far as the fiercely defended heights around the Kreuzberg Pass formed the front which hardly moved throughout the war years in spite of constant attacks and counterattacks with shocking losses on both sides. Italy declared war on Austria-Hungary on 23rd May 1915 and on 24th May Italian soldiers already occupied the heights of the Carnic ridge, though equally unexpectedly regiments of the German Alpine Corps from Bavaria arrived with two battalions a

day later on 25th May. The Germans were not yet at war with Italy. On the same day the Italians captured the weakly-defended Cima Frugnoni, the Pfannspitze and the Porze. Basically there were two means of penetrating the Austrian lines: either across the relatively low 1,360 m (4,462 ft) Plöcken Pass or via the 1,636 m (5,367 ft) Kreuzbergsattel pass. The Italians attacked both with such vehemence that the terrible losses made this one of the bloodiest battles in the Alpine war. The adversaries were often only a few metres apart sheltering in hastily dug trenches.

This front sector also brought forth popular heroes. Their deeds did not affect the general war situation but have gone down in history and popular legend. Such as the farmer Stremitzer and ingeneous Karl Prusik who managed to capture a small rock on the Wolyerkopf just a few metres from the enemy, or the district police chief Simon Steinberger who took the Cellon in a surprise attack, or the volunteer militia, the Kärntner Schützen who worked for eight weeks burrowing a 780 m long tun-

Above centre: Italian prisoners of war on the Elfer in the Sexten Dolomites. Right: in the Cinque Torri area the NCO Edoardo Turkheimer has his beard shaved. He is well provided for, with a walking stick and wash basin in front of the tent.

nel through the snow towards the Italian customs house in spring 1917 with the intention of surprising the troops guarding the border. The Italians defended their positions courageously, there were dead on both sides, the Austrians had to retreat through their snow tunnel just as quickly as they had come. Still the memory of their exploits lives on, like many others.

The Dolomite front

It was the magnificence of these mountains which quickly turned these valleys into a world-wide tourist attraction in the 19th century. The peaks had already been conquered before the war, while the valleys subsequently attracted holidaymakers in search of pure air, curative waters, though also adventurers, explorers and with them the aristocracy. Railways were built and an impressive road even crossed the Dolomite passes. When Italy declared war on Austria many people turned their attention to this region which they knew from their travels. For strategic purposes the village of Cortina d' Ampezzo, the unproclaimed

capital of the Dolomites, was abandoned to the enemy without a fight, a moral-boosting godsend for the Italians. However, cruel disillusionment soon followed. They were unable to push forward, soon nobody believed any more in a fast advance on Vienna. Shortly after the outset of hostilities the mountain guide Sepp Innerkofler from Sexten fell on the Paternkofel on 4th July 1915. Too old at 54 to be called up for active service, he fought in the Standschützen. However what followed was stalemate rather than a modern military campaign. This conflict in the high regions of rock is remembered above all for the many daring and risky actions which took place on both sides, for example the first storming of the Sextner Rotwand by Italian troops, or the capture of the Serauta ridge gap in the Marmolata area. It became fixed in people's souls leaving lasting reminders in the mountain faces and summits which were simply blasted away, including the Col di Lana, the Lagazuoi, the Schreckenstein, and of course the memory of the thousands who were swept to their

Kaiserjäger-Museum Berg-Isel, Innsbruck (2)

Above left: an Austrian position in the rocks on the Lagazuoi. Above right: building of living quarters in the Tre Sassi area. We still marvel at the spectacular logistical achievements of those times.

deaths by avalanches during the war winter of 1915-1916. In places up to twelve metres (40 feet) of snow fell. Around 300 deaths were caused by a single avalanche on the Gran Poz in the Marmolada area, almost as many in a another deadly avalanche catastrophe in the Höhlenstein Valley.

Viktoria Savs fought in the Drei Zinnen area disguised as a man. She was a small, petite girl who was determined to play here part on the front line. Here right leg was crushed in a rockfall and had to be amputated below the knee. It was only in the field hospital at Sillian that the 16-year-old Viktor Savs turned out to be in fact Viktoria. She was decorated several times for bravery and lived until the ripe old age of 80. Anton von Tschurtschenthaler stood his ground tenaciously on the Col di Lana, even when it was blasted away by Italian troops on 17th April, 1916. This mountain went down in history as the bloody mountain. In an audacious action Italo Lunelli, Giovanni Sala and Antonio Berti captured the Sentinella ridge gap near the Sextner Rotwand. Even at this

point it became apparent that the ethnic Italians in Trentino, at that time the southernmost part Tyrol, were torn between allegiances. The Austrian Italo Lunelli fought on the Italian side under the name Raffaele Da Basso. There was a further ethnic minority in the Dolomites with their own language, the Ladins, who were likewise distrusted by Austrians, while the Italians found their loyalty to the Monarchy baffling.

The Marmolada, the highest summit in the Dolomites became legendary. In the wake of battles with mounting casualties the Austrian engineer Leo Handl had the ingenious idea of building a network of tunnels through the glacier. In this way entire citadels came into being in the ice. This enabled supplies and reinforcements to be brought up to the high regions unhindered and soldiers were better protected against severe weather and avalanches. Even before burrowing in the ice had begun work was underway excavating tunnels extending for hundreds of kilometres in the hard Dolomite rock. Almost immediately the mountains, the Paternkofel, the

Archivio arch. Fabio Ortolani, Foto cap. Achille Rosica

Above right: an Italian officer poses with an unexploded shell. This war consumed enormous quantities of valuable materials made of iron and copper. Even church bells were melted for this purpose.

Tofana, the Lagazuoi were in many places penetrated by networks of galleries. Here, too, the Italians were unable to achieve any significant breakthrough. Finally the crushing defeat suffered by the Italians at Carporetto resulted in their troops being withdrawn from the entire Dolomite front, and so a third winter of fighting in these mountains was averted.

The Vicenza Alps

A front line had developed in the form of a triangle from Val Sugana westwards to the Adige Valley with the important towns of Trento and Bolzano/Bozen well in the Austrian rear. This area of high plateaux, peaks and valleys witnessed the horrors of war unfold at their most hideous. Heinz von Lichem wrote of combat on Monte Pasubio, a extensive massif to the east of Rovereto: "That was hell on earth: mines, raging avalanches, constant hand-to-hand fighting, soldiers vegetating wretchedly under arctic conditions in the depths of winter." In this area both the Italians and Austrians had built strong defences – seemingly intended to

last forever. However, once fighting started in earnest the two sides preferred to retreat to their much safer shelters in hastily-blasted caverns in the rocks. The fortified positions on the Austrian side, Verle, Lusern, Geschwendt, Cherle and Serrada faced the Italian forts Verena, Campolungo, Casa Ratti and Campomolon. The high plateau of the 'Sette Comuni' or 'Seven Villages' was fortified to protect the Austro-Hungarian Empire against a possible Italian breakthrough into the Adige Valley and to defend South Tyrol. This expanse of highland saw the launch in spring 1916 of the so-called 'Strafexpedition' or 'Punitive Campaign', a name invented by the Italians to strike fear into their own people. The aim was for the Austrians to break through the south-eastern Val Sugana defences and penetrate deep into Italian territory, a counteroffensive of Austria-Hungary to wreak vengeance on their perfidious partners who had torn up a long-standing treaty of friendship and sold out to the highest bidder in the hope of obtaining territory at Austria's expense. This plan was to be accomplished with the help of German troops. However it ended in a fiasco: the German ranks on the Western Front had lost vast numbers of soldiers fighting at Verdun. The dead there needed to be replaced, while in Russia General Brussilow had started a huge offensive, causing havoc on the Eastern Front. Austrian troops were needed more urgently elsewhere and so this 'Punitive Campaign' ended ingloriously in June 1916. On 16th June 1916 the chief of staff Con-

Museo Storico Trento B 12 287

The Italian fort Verena bombarded by Austro-Hungarian troops.

tenant Pivko and several of his countrymen and after several weeks of planning – in taking this outpost. The Italians wore Austrian uniforms, knew the German passwords and were thus able to take advantage of surprise to break in and entrench themselves. It was only after fierce fighting that the Austrians managed to dislodge the foreign defenders. Bitter conflicts raged everywhere in this area. On 10th June 1917 the Italians attacked the positions of Ortigara on the 'Seven Villages' high plateau with 1,500 pieces of artillery, though after 19 days of attacks and counterattacks and useless sacrifice nothing was gained.

Monte Corno to the east of Rovereto on the other hand attained doubtful renown, for it was here in July 1916 that the irredentist Cesare Battisti was taken prisoner following a bold but unfortunate attack by the Italians. Cesare Battisti came from

rad von Hötzendorf gave the order to halt the offensive and on 18th June even ordered his troops to retreat to their well-defended positions from where the campaign had started.

The position of Carzano in the Valsugana valley has taken its place in the annals of this war because the Italians succeeded – partially through cunning and partially through betrayal by the Czech First lieu-

Trento. He had received a doctorate from the University of Innsbruck, had studied in Graz, Florence and Turin, and had been elected to the National Assembly in Vienna in the service of Austria. In spite of being an Austrian subject Battisti had joined the Italian army at the beginning of the war. Immediately after his capture he was condemned to death at Trento after a show trial on 13th July 1916. He quickly became a martyr in the eyes of the Italians, while the Austrians despised him for being as a deserter and saboteur.

With its two main summits the Pasubio towers like a 2,250 metre high fortress. Whoever managed to completely control this high plateau could command the Adige Valley between Trento and Verona as well as large areas of the northern Italian Alpine Foothills. After bitter and bloody struggles the Austrians and Italians each occupied one the two summits. The Austrians blew up the Italian positions here in the largest explosion in this Alpine war, an event which cost the lives of 2,000 Italian soldiers in 1917. There was nowhere for soldiers to easily entrench themselves in the limestone rock, each trench and dugout had to be laboriously blasted into the rock. Relentless wind and storms raged across the region, and to make matters worse the winter was the most awful in living memory. Then from November 1917 until the end of the war Monte Grappa took Monte Pasubio's place as the mountain of horrors. Italy's strength was seriously sapped in the wake of a devastating defeat in the 12th Battle of the Isonzo. Troops retreated disorderly, left enormous quantities of artillery behind and Italy only struggled to its feet

again after asking for support from her British and French allies. The war had now moved on from these dreadful, hostile mountain summits into the lowlands and plains. There the Italians proved more effective adversaries. By the first days of November 1917 the battle-tried Italian Alpine troops (Alpini) and light infantry (Bersaglieri) which had been transferred south from the Dolomite front were already entrenched on Monte Grappa, the Asalone and Monte Tomba. In spite of constant as-

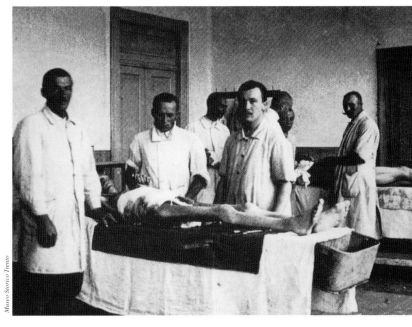

Museo Storico Trento

A soldier is treated in the hospital at Levico. Emaciation and symptoms of malnutrition are clearly visible.

saults by Austrian troops the Italian positions held and the beleaguered army even began to make unexpected gains. Once they were fighting on Italian soil defending their home country the Italians proved formidable adversaries in the way the Kärnten and Tyrolean defenders had when protecting their own villages two years earlier.

The war around Lake Garda

A part of Trentino to the west of the river Adige survived relatively unscathed from the war. It comprises the Giudicarie Valleys and the Brenta Dolomites (now famous for the ski resort Madonna di

Exposed Italian cabins on the Corno di Lagoscuro in the area of the Tonale Pass.

Campiglio), bordered to the north by Adamello massif, and the region of Lake Garda to the south. In this theatre the Italians never planned to overcome the Austrian troops even though Lake Garda at an elevation of only 67 metres above sea level was the lowest point in this Alpine war. There were occasional mock battles, even half-hearted assaults, though otherwise

troops which were assigned to protect the fortifications in this region lived out the war in relative safety. The actual fierce front action in this theatre took place farther north towards the glacier regions of the Presena and the Adamello massif with its peak at 3,554 metres elevation.

The glacier war in the Adamello massif

Throughout the history of mankind protracted wars had never been fought in Alpine glacier regions, though this changed dramatically when the expanses of eternal ice in the Adamello and Ortler massifs were transformed into a theatre of battle. The Tonale Pass was strategically important for both the Italians and Austrians. From there it was possible to penetrate into Lombardy and take control of its industrial centres, while on the Trentino side the town of Trento could be reached via the Val di Non and the victor could have significantly shortened this section of the front. For this reason from 1860 onwards the area surrounding the Tonale Pass had been extensively fortified. After a hesitating start to the war both sides soon concentrated their main efforts on fighting pitched battles for control of the highest-lying glaciated summits. Unlike the Dolomite theatre there were no mountain roads, well-built cart tracks or footpaths in the region between the Adamello and the Ortler. A ten-hour march was often necessary to carry the most urgently needed supplies up to the high positions.

The very first battle in the history of warfare to be fought in glaciated terrain took place on 9th June 1915 on the Presena Glacier. The battle also saw the very first bold attacks by soldiers on skis. At the outset of the war the Italians had carelessly

Museo della Guerra Bianca, Temù

20

abandoned the Passo Paradiso and the Monticello ridge, giving the Austrians the advantage of being able to occupy these positions from where they had a commanding view of the deployment area on the Tonale and through the Val Camonica. A grave mistake which the Italians sought to rectify. However the first glacier battle in history ended in victory for the Austrian Kaiserschützen.

On 15th July 1915 the Austrian troops set out to take the weakly defended refuge Rifugio Garibaldi, full of confidence and certain of success. Surprisingly for all sides the assault was repulsed. From then on this mountain refuge became the Italian hub for all hostilities. Fighting came to a halt in the glacier regions during the winter of 1915-1916 with soldiers venturing onto the summits occasionally only to clear snow or to make sporadic reconnaissance tours. It was regarded as impossible to carry out strategic warfare there during the winter months. However during the following winters this attitude changed on both sides. In the Ortler and Adamello area the highest summits and strategic positions even at elevations beyond three thousand metres were fortified into winterised bulwarks. In contrast to the area between the Julian Alps as far as the Val Sugana where, in the wake of the lost battle of the Isonzo there was no fighting in the high mountains during the third winter of 1917-1918, in this area soldiers had to endure three fiendish winters with metres-high snowfall and temperatures down to minus 40 degrees centigrade.

The bell tolled for Calvi brothers in April 1916. In a daring attack requiring extensive mountain climbing Captain Nino Calvi seized control of the area from Lob-

bia Alta to Monte Fumo. At the end of April the valiant Lieutenant Attilio Calvi was ordered to attack the line from Crozzon di Folgorida as far as the Passo di Cavento, dressed in normal grey-green military uniforms. A fatal mistake on the glacier: Attilio Calvi and his men were

Foto-Leo Bährendt. Archiv Konrad Knoll

Soldiers trudge uphill towards the Ortler summit. With its 3,905 metre high summit this mountain went down in history as the highest battleground ever.

picked off by the Austrian marksmen as if at a shooting contest. The 13th December 1916 went down in the history of this high mountain war as the 'Black St. Lucia Day'. All of a sudden twelve metres of fresh snow fell, followed by a thaw, the perfect recipe for devastating avalanches. Over the next few days thousands on both sides were swept to their deaths, often up to one hundred men per avalanche.

Two moving events took place in 1917. On 15th June the offensive began for the strategically important 3,402 metres-high Corno di Cavento. It was initially taken by the Italians, then almost precisely a year later the Austro-Hungarian troops captured it in hand-to-hand fighting and with heavy losses. The soldiers had dug a long

Museo della Guerra Bianca, Temù

The year is 1921. Gaunt widows and sad war orphans kneel in the military cemetery of Pezzo in the area of the Stilfser Joch pass.

tunnel through the ice and snow and managed to completely surprise the well-entrenched Alpini units. However the Corno di Cavento was soon retaken by the Italians on 19th July 1918.

On 27th September 1917 the venerable village Ponte di Legno in Val Camonica was burnt to the ground. The Austrian troops hit it with firebombs and heavy artillery as

retribution for the shelling of some of their ammunition dumps in the Tonale area.

The Ortler region

At an altitude of 3,902 metres the peak of the Ortler was Austria's highest mountain. Throughout the history of mankind a summit at this elevation had never been a theatre of sustained combat. Italians and Austrians fought on these heights for over three years, undertook bold and courageous coups, while the seemingly impossible feats they performed in hauling heavy artillery up to the mountain tops and ridges still command enormous respect. Two powerful 10.5 cm guns were laboriously drawn first of all from Gomagoi to Sulden and from there via the Payerhütte refuge up to the summit area of the Ortler massif. From there 30 mountain guides and 30 Russian prisoners of war dragged the dismantled guns up to the peak in an act of superhuman exertion.

The capture of the 3,859 metre high Königsspitze is also the stuff of legends. In spring 1917 the Italians and Austrians both decided almost simultaneously to occupy this summit which they deemed strategically important. Neither side knew of the other's intentions as the soldiers set out on their mission. The Kaiserschützen were a day faster than the Alpini, though this did not prevent the two sides from entrenching themselves 150 metres apart.

The story of the capture of the Hoher Schneid, a 3,434 metre high summit in the Ortler massif is even stranger. The first to occupy the peak were the Italians in October 1916, from where they immediately trained their machinegun fire onto the Austrian positions. A breathtaking assault plan was drawn up. The soldiers began to dig a two kilometre-long tunnel in the ice to a position just beneath the Italian line. They worked day and night under top secrecy using hoes, picks and shovels. At temperatures around minus six centigrade, suffering continuously from oxygen starvation and constantly having to contend with the problem of disposing of the 4,000 cubic metres of ice without raising suspicion, the men drew close to the Italian troops. Then the incredible happened: nobody realised how close they were to their objective and the Alpini suspected nothing. On 17th March 1917 while the working party was taking a midday break an Italian soldier suddenly broke through the thin layer of ice and fell into the tunnel. The decision to attack was taken hurriedly with the aim of dislodging the nonplussed Italian summit team with a heavy hand grenade attack. All the same little changed on this front over the years apart from minimal territorial gains and alternations in the occupation of certain summits.

The end

The end came unexpectedly and remarkably. In October 1918 the revitalised Italians were pushing forward to the decisive battle supported by allied troops. The Austrian army stood with its back to the wall and were at the end of their tether. Events moved quickly: on 30th October 1918 Austria asked for an armistice. The Trentino was threatened in a pincer movement across the Tonale Pass as well as from Monte Grappa. On 2nd November Italy agreed to a truce to come into effect at midnight on 3rd November. The Austrian troops were hurriedly informed. However the news leaked out that the armistice was not to come into effect until 3 p.m. on 4th November. Thousands of Austrians rushing back to their lines were taken prisoner. The Austrian

These women in Trentino begin the work of reconstruction amid the ruins of their houses.

Empire collapsed and a new world order came into being. The seeds for the Second World War and for many other intractable problems were sown.

Michael Wachtler

A historical document: a massive rock 200 metres high and 140 metres wide thunders down from the Lagazuoi, the result of the Austrians detonating a mine on 22nd May 1917. Beforehand Austrian soldiers had excavated a tunnel, filled it with 30,000 kg of

explosives, then detonated it. On the Col di Lana on the other hand it was the Italians who blew up the summit. Nevertheless even these peaks of technical ingeniousness were harassing tactics rather than strategies which determined the war's outcome.

25

Wien, Heeresgeschichtliches Museum

The aged emperor Franz Josef began to prepare for war and reckoned with the unconditional support of Germany.

A completely different war

Sunday 28th June 1914 was a typical summer's day in the Balkans - blistering. For the Serbs it was St. Vitus day. It memorialized the Battle of Kosovo in 1389 where the Serbs were defeated by Turkey. The heir to the Austro-Hungarian throne, Archduke Franz Ferdinand with his consort Sophie and their enormous retinue were visiting Sarajevo on occasion of their wedding anniversary. Theirs was a morganatic marriage and in Vienna Sophie would never have been allowed to ride in the same car as her husband. But this was Sarajevo. Serbia was a hotbed of nationalistic intrigue and the royal visit could be seen by some almost as a provocation. An initial warning was a close call. On their drive from the railway station to the City Hall a bomb was hurled at the Archduke's car and lightly injured passengers in the third car, Lieutenant Colonel Merizzi, Count Boos-Waldeck and Sophie's attendant, Countess Lanjus. Undaunted, the Archduke continued to the city hall for a reception with the mayor Fehim Effendi Curcic, who had been riding in the front car, and councillors. Curcic was unaware of the occurrence due to the noise of the cars. The furious Archduke interrupted the mayor 's welcome speech, seizing him by the arm: "One comes here to visit and is received with bombs. Mr. Mayor, what do you say? It's outrageous!" The Archduke calmed down during the speech. Afterwards he expressed his wish to visit the bomb victims, but the car his chauffer was following took a wrong turn at Imperial Bridge and had to stop and turn around. At this point the assassin Gavrilo Princip, one of seven conspirators acted quickly and precisely, drawing his Browning handgun and firing twice before the car could complete its turn. They were the shots which were to kindle the tinderbox of the First World War, a conflagration which swept aside centuries-old political powers and royal dynasties,

Above left: The last day of peace. The Austrian heir to the throne, Franz Ferdiand D´Este, heir to the Austro-Hungarian throne and his consort drive through Sarajevo on 28th June, 1914. Below left: The Bosnian-Serb Gavrilo Princip is arrested, narrowly rescued from a lynch mob. It emerged that the Serbian 'Black Hand', the group which supported him and provided the weapons were high military officers and other Serbian patriots. Above right: The blood-soaked uniform which Arch Duke Franz Ferdinand was wearing on the day of his assassination is kept as a relic in the War Museum in Vienna. Below right: The corpses lying in state.

heralding in a new epoch. Thousands have tried to explain the reasons for this war which left Europe in ruins and sowed the seeds for the next world war. Perhaps Robert Musil expresses it most eloquently and impartially. Musil, one of the 20th century's greatest writers was himself a veteran of the Dolomite front and later publisher of the 'Tiroler Soldatenzeitung' (Tyrolean Solders' Newspaper) in Bozen. The author of the momentous work 'The Man Without Qualities' discerned the general loss of values and all-pervading tedium of life, the dreadful stagnation which had descended upon Europe. "In 1914 people were literally bored to death,

so the war came amid a fever of adventure and the allurement of distant, undiscovered shores." Men were even grateful to sacrifice their lives, to die in order for their memories to live on in glory.

The shots of Sarajevo were a liberation, at last the chance had come to fundamentally change the world. For another great contemporary writer, Franz Kafka, the start of the war passed as if it was of no concern to him. Austria had declared war on Serbia on 2nd August 1914 and Germany was about to do the same, when Kafka wrote in his diary: "Germany has declared war on Russia. – Afternoon swimming lessons."

Museo Storico, Trento

Günther Obwegs, Gottfried Leitgeb

A cheerful, optimistic start

Left: Trento 1914. Hostilities commence in a distant country. Men are called to arms. Enthusiasm still prevails, given that the war is universally expected to be short. Right: A Landsturm (Territorial Army) battalion with their obsolete weapons. It soon became apparent that this would be the first modern war fought with state-of-the-art weapons far more fearsome than mankind had ever known before. There are dozens upon dozens of such photos showing men departing from every village and town. The grim reality of the war first hit home when more and more troops had to be called up to replace the fallen.

Günther Obwegs, Gottfried Leitgeb

Museo Storico, Trento

Left: Fritz and Alois Berger, father and son have their photo taken together for the last time to immortalise their memory. Like the two Alpini soldiers who apparently aren't sure what the war is all about. Both photos express the profound fear of an indeterminable and ominous time.

Istituto Culturale Ladin   *Istituto Culturale Ladin*

All rivers flow into disaster

Left: Because of the changed political circumstances many Tyroleans belonging to the Ladin and Italian ethnic groups took refuge in Austria, where makeshift camps were hastily built to accommodate them, or they were interned there against their will. Above all for the Ladin and Italian speaking inhabitants the situation was extremely difficult for a number of reasons. Others were interned in camps in Italy. Right: Photo taken in Reichenburg, Bohemia shows Ladin children learning to read and write.

Loris Lancedelli

Like numerous villages along the southern mountain front Cortina d'Ampezzo was abandoned to the Italians without a fight. Italian chaplains immediately took over the deserted churches, while teachers instructed children in 'objective and unadulterated' Italian history.

Museo della Guerra, Rovereto *Loris Lancedelli, Foto sottoten. Almachilde Chiarini*

Mountains became fortresses

Left: Makeshift camps were built even in the most exposed places, like here on the Lagazuoi. Right: These positions were subsequently improved, fortified and even made 'winter-proof'. Supply lines and logistics posed enormous problems for the warring parties. These photos communicate an idea of the daring acts carried out in an attempt to gain decisive terrain, almost all of which failed.

Michael Wachtler

In 1916 a winter storm transformed the camp on the Würzbach mountain beside the Sexten Rotwand into a bizarre fairytale landscape. A romantic snapshot for posterity but a hard struggle against nature for all soldiers who had to hold out in such high places.

Michael Wachtler

Günther Obwegs-Gottfried Leitgeb

A deadly game

Martial aplomb featured prominently. In the animal world it is called display behaviour. Many pictures from the time show the extent to which humans are different. Left: An Italian officer with a breast plate. "It is sweet to die for the fatherland" was an often-used slogan. To think differently was treachery.

Marco Zardini

Many 'action' photographs were actually posed. They were copied for families of soldiers and also for the media in various forms and with various captions to depict a frenetic appetite for battle.

31

Günther Obwegs-Gottfried Leitgeb

Istituto Cultural Ladin - Vigo di Fassa

Careworn faces

Even today we find photographs such as these moving. In addition to the lasting pictorial reminder they reveal the subjects' innermost feelings, like this elderly farmer going to war as a volunteer Standschütze (left), leaving his wife at home, and the Italian soldier (right), lost in thought while reading. It is only on closer examination that many details of the depth of human feelings and heartache become apparent.

Tiroler Kaiserjägermuseum - Innsbruck

The 1st Tyrolean Kaiserjäger Regiment in the Dolomites. Lost in thought, an officer looks at photographs of his loved ones with diffused light seeping in from the outside. Each day brought fresh bad news which soldiers had to come to terms with.

Museum 1915-18 Kötschach-Mauthen
Museo della Guerra Bianca, Temù

How could anyone endure this?

Left: The famous and notorious 'Doghouse' near the Sexten Rotwand. It is hard to imagine that men actually had to lived in there. Right: A long and extremely precarious rope bridge on the 'Bocchetta del Gendarme di Casamadre' on the Adamello. The element of adventure and constant diversity differentiate these pictures from those taken on the Western and Eastern fronts.

Museo Storico, Trento
Museo della Guerra Bianca, Temù

Left: A soldier and his comrade labour across the Cima d'Asta in the Val di Fiemme. A camp on the western wall of the Corno di Cavento (m. 3402) on the Adamello. This mountain idyll has been made perilous by an autumn storm. Each false step could be deadly.

Arch. Fabio Ortolani, Foto A. De Marinis

Tiroler Soldatenzeitung

Weapons previously unknown in warfare

Left: Italian soldiers poke fun at an unexploded Austrian shell. Right: Two Austrian soldiers proudly pose for a photograph on a 420 artillery piece. Tonnes of metal were fired and the shortage of raw materials resulted in church bells being melted down. Even private households were asked to donate metal.

Arch. M. Turkheimer, Foto E. Turkheimer

Kriegsarchiv Wien

An artillery position camouflaged with mountain pine branches in the Ampezzo Dolomites. The two dogs belonging to the NCO Edoardo Turkheimer distract from the deadly threat of these weapons. This soldier has put on a gas mask to guard against the possibility of a poison gas attack.

Leo Bährendt, Archiv Konrad Knoll

Superhuman feats

Dozens of Austrian soldiers haul logs uphill in the Ortler region to build positions in the summit areas. Russian prisoners of war were often used. Escape was impossible here in such rough, virtually impassable terrain, though hopes of a breaking through to the Italian positions were likewise slim. This picture shows the everyday grind and toil which sapped men's strength even behind the lines.

Konrad Knoll, Foto Otto Bährendt

Museo della Guerra, Peio

Left: An Austro-Hungarian soldier obviously unaccustomed to mountain terrain is hauled up by comrades in the Ortler massif. A group was usually only as strong as its weakest link. Right: Two soldiers climb up a vertical face on the Cevedale.

Museo della Guerra Bianca, Temù

Museo della Guerra Bianca, Temù

The icy power of winter

The first winter of the war had been underestimated by all. However, lessons were learnt quickly. Left: A group of Alpini solders trudge uphill on the Adamello. They are wearing white camouflage suits to avoid being spotted by the enemy. The Italians have erected a tent camp in the Conca Mandrone hollow beneath the Presena-Spitze.

Museo Storico, Trento

Museo della Guerra, Peio

Left: An Italian assault in the mountains. Right: The Ortler and the Adamello close to the Swiss border, along with the Marmolada in the Dolomites were the highest theatres of battle during the First World War. Thousands fell prey to avalanches or bad equipment.

36

Tiroler Kaiserjägermuseum - Innsbruck

Istituto Cultural Ladin - Vigo di Fassa

The destructive forces of man and nature

Edifices and historical monuments which took centuries to build were destroyed and lost forever in minutes. Not even religious buildings were left unscathed. And for the first time men even ventured to destructive power on nature. Mountains were blown up with tonnes of explosives. Left: The ruins of the church of Pieve di Cadore. Right: A Ladin family amid the rubble of their house.

Museo Storico, Trento

Museo Storico, Trento

Left: A night time explosion on the Pasubio mountain. Right: An Italian shell explodes on the Cima Vezzena. None of the massive explosions, whether on the Lagazuoi, on the Pasubio or Col di Lana was decisive for the outcome of the war; nevertheless they earned their place in history.

Museo Storico Santa Lucia

Raffaele Grammendola, Foto Alfredo Grammendola

A little laughter, vale of tears

Left: A game of table tennis beneath the Passo Giau and a snowball fight at the foot of the Tofana (right). Men did whatever they could to forget the monotonous routine of everyday life. Soldiers had no rights and anyone who refused to obey orders was charged with treason. These pictures are snapshots of the inner world of ordinary people and not of the military.

Istituto Cultural Ladin - Vigo di Fassa

Museo Storico, Trento B 14/649

Left: Men taking a communal bath in the Val di Fassa. Right: A game of chess on the Elferkofel in the Sexten Dolomites. Any distraction from the mundane routine of every-day life, the daily struggle for survival far from one's home, family and children was welcome.

Museo della Guerra Bianca, Temù, Augusto Materzanini

Museo Storico Trento

The last-ditch stand

Left and right: Unusual methods of transport and remarkable cargoes. Two soldiers on the Adamello shun the long and arduous march, while the donkey does not seem to dislike being saved the long way down to the valley.

Tiroler Kaiserjägermuseum - Innsbruck

"Not fallen in honour on the field of battle – Southern Front 1917". Even though daily life was so deadly serious, anyone who could bring a smile to men's faces was immensely popular. Like the author of this picture, providing a snapshot of the kind of humour which prevailed in spite of the hardships men had to endure.

Tiroler Kaiserjägermuseum - Innsbruck

Museo della Guerra Bianca, Temù

Where is God?

Nowhere did men search for God so desperately than in the most remote places and amid sheer rock faces. Left: An Austro-Hungarian soldiers' solemn Christmas celebration and right an artistic ice altar crafted by Italian troops on the Passo della Lobbia Alta in the Adamello area.

Leo Bährendt, Archiv Konrad Knoll

Tiroler Kaiserjägermuseum - Innsbruck

Left: A military chaplain says mass in the Ortler massif. Each soldier prays to God in his own way. Right: There were few holidays on the front which induced both sides to silence their weapons, even for a few hours, out of a longing for peace.

Loris Lancedelli

Gütnher Ohwegs, Gottfried Leitgeb

Together but divided

The longer the war went on, the greater were the chasms which opened everywhere. War-weariness was rife, as well as a silent hatred of the powers that be. Left: An Italian Red Cross nurse at work. Right: A small celebration in honour of the medical chief of staff. The legendary Austrian doctor Lorenz Böhler worked in Bozen (Bolzano) and on the Dolomite front.

Col. Gianni Bellò, Foto ten. Ettore Boschi

Museo Storico, Trento B 14/649

Left: Everyday life for troops in the Ampezzo Dolomites. In the army special emphasis was placed on the subjugation of an individual's free will and thoughts. Right: Trento. Jewish soldiers from countries ruled by the Austrian monarchy in the soldiers' canteen. Some years later part of the blame for the war was heaped upon them.

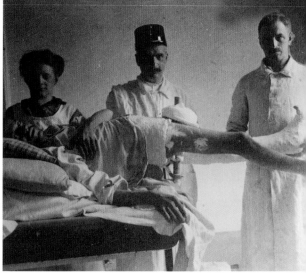

Foto Leo Bährendt, Archiv Konrad Knoll

We were promised the world

Left: The very last food is requisitioned from the farmsteads. Right: The hospitals quickly filled up with wounded. The very young and elderly had been sent to war. In the end even that proved insufficient. The desire to somehow escape with one's own life became increasingly a soldier's main concern.

Istituto Cultural Ladin - Vigo di Fassa

Foto Leo Bährendt, Archiv Konrad Knoll

Left: "The constantly diminishing food supplies provided the basis for a farce" is the caption given to this photo by a soldier in the Val di Fassa. Right: The war turned even those who had never smoked beforehand into chain smokers. Cigarettes united, made men courageous and suppressed hunger, fear and psychological tension.

42

Il piccione è pronto per partire

Museo della Guerra, Peio

Museo Storico, Trento

The yearning for peace

People had expected the final photos of this war to turn out differently. They were characterised by tears of sorrow rather than joy, for in the end the victors were those who were just a tiny bit stronger among the tottering. Left: An Austrian officer plays affectionately with an eagle. Right: During the war pigeons worked as postmen. The dove of peace was unwelcome.

Museo Storico, Trento

Museo Storico, Trento b 13/306

Left: Laying down of arms. The weapons fell silent at the beginning of November 1918, like here in Trento. While in Bozen men struggled to catch the train to Austria. Four years earlier they had set out on the same trains full of optimism, while here the gaunt soldiers storm the wagons taking them into an uncertain future.

Mountains are simply blasted away

Throughout the world there are few mountains which have been so mistreated by the hand of man compared with the Dolomites. At the outset of the First World War troops on both sides took up positions and became so well entrenched on the summits that neither side could gain a metre of ground. Then came a brilliant idea: simply to blow up these mountain colossuses. With the most primitive tunnelling equipment, covered in dust, almost blind and suffering from rheumatism men worked for months on end excavating galleries in the hard dolomite rock. Finally after tens, hundreds of metres they hollowed

out a main chamber beneath the enemy's position which was then slowly filled with massive quantities of explosives, in some cases over 30 tonnes. On each occasion the blast was a secret celebration, watches were synchronised, the exact time of the encounter with the enemy kept top secret, while diversionary and disruptive tactics were employed in succession. People, 'The Enemy' were blown up with the mountain. 17th April, 1916: Lieutenant Don Gelasio Caetani, Prince of Sermoneta and his men were waiting restlessly in the gallery christened Santa Giulia beneath the Col di Lana. They crouched in the cramped recesses in the rock, packed like sardines waiting for the great moment. Then a messenger rushed up to him at 11.30 pm with the long awaited order: "Your Honour, you are to detonate the mine at 11.35. The Commander on the Col di Lana. Signed Mezzetti." Those five minutes seemed like an eternity. The engineers had been working feverishly since 13th January 1916, excavating the tunnel deep into the mountain, 52 metres long (105 metres counting its secondary galleries) with a gradient of 15 degrees. All attempts at taking the strategically crucial mountain by infantry assaults had failed (from the summit the Austrians could observe all Italian troop movements, besides it was an obstacle to their advance towards the Pustertal valley), and so the Italians decided to try blowing up the summit position. Engineers had worked day and night in eight-hour shifts, many attracted by a premium. They were paid 50 to 100 lire based on the progress of the work to incentivise maximum speed. The gallery had been perfectly calculated to stop four metres beneath the Austrian position. On the advice of the experienced Colonel D'Ippoliti the

Adolf Moroder

Below: On the Col di Lana. Even when there was a lull in the fighting there was no respite. Positions had to be put back into working order after each attack or cleared after snowfall.

Michael Wachtler

The Col di Lana on the day of the explosion (left) and immediately after the blast.
The event brought notoriety to this unassuming mountain. During the war some
18,000 soldiers either lost their lives here or were wounded.

tunnel was then filled with explosives. 300 soldiers toiled carrying 5 tonnes of solidified nitro-glycerine the long way up the tunnel. The final hours of this madness became like a descent into hell. The commander of the sappers, Lieutenant Maggio, collapsed after three hours as a result of the poisonous gases created by the glycerine. As a result Gelasio Caetani was completely alone in command. 31 men formed a chain, the air was stale and filled with poisonous fumes. Slowly the ventilator provided a little relief. It is hard to imagine what would have happened if he too had become incapacitated. The engineers toiled for 50 hours under the strictest secrecy.

Meanwhile the Austrian Kaiserjäger soldiers had a foreboding of the danger: the spectre of the summit being blown up robbed them of their spirit and they were powerless to prevent it. For days they had heard the sound of hammering and chiselling beneath them, suspected what was happening but there was too little time to construct a counter gallery. All they could do was wait and, with meticulous measures, prepare for the worst. Destiny had to run its course. Death lurked a few metres beneath them. The unanswered question was, who would providence spare and who would meet his terrible end there? The mountain would erupt spewing forth fire on a certain

day at a certain moment, finally to collapse taking with it all the occupying soldiers. The burden of responsibility and accountability on the officers in command at the time was enormous. The disaster was to hit the 5th and 6th companies who manned the position in three-day shifts. During the night of 12th to 13th April Adalbert Homa and the 86 men of his 5th company trudged up to the position to relieve the defenders, so they were destined to escape the horror of that fatal night.

The soldiers were aware of what was coming – the boring noises had been audible since mid March - but accepted their fate without complaint, content to sacrifice their lives for their country. No more boring noises had been heard since the evening of 14th April and the Austrians reckoned that it would take the Italians a good 48 hours to load the mine and blow their position away together with the summit of the Col di Lana. On the night of 16th to 17th April Homa's 5th company was relieved by First Lieutenant Anton Tschurtschenthaler's 6th company of the 2nd Kaiserjäger regiment. Homa had often discussed his foreboding with his men, prepared them for what was coming and sent a messenger down to the command post warning them to refrain from sending up Tschurtschenthaler's company to relieve them. However, the messenger

45

Michael Wachtler

A gallery is excavated in the dolomite rock in the area of the Cinque Torri. The same task is carried out by an Austrian sapper on the Lagazuoi.

was wounded on a ridge pathway and fell to his death before the warning could be delivered. The psychological agitation and tension among the men reached fever pitch. Nobody had slept for two days and each did what he could to compose himself in the knowledge that the explosives a few feet beneath could be detonated at any moment. Those manning the fire trenches were given roborants, for everyone knew they were in the greatest danger: an explosion would mean certain death for them. The Italians had spent two nights getting their ranges and preparing for the attack, all approach routes had been blocked and no supplies could get through. The soldiers had to resort to their emergency rations, snow was melted for water, the wood from the shattered cable car station used as fuel. The fire trenches were a pile of rubble, forward shelters had to be evacuated. Everybody expected the explosion to occur on the night of 16th and 17th April. Harassing drumfire reached a climax. Then just after 9 pm the Italian artillery fell silent. The night was then relatively quiet.

The hours went by without any significant occurrences, then the piquets noticed men creeping up from the Sief Saddle in the direction of the Col di Lana. Were they their own troops? Had they not received the message warning them not to come? First Lieutenant Anton Tschurtschenthaler appeared with his company. He had not received any message, the messenger had not arrived. The relief went smoothly and took three hours, until 5 am. Finally the officers and NCOs made their tense farewells. Captain Adalbert Homa took von Tschurtschenthaler's hand a last time and held it firm and long, then took his leave certain that he would never see his comrade again. Soon afterwards the Italians began to fire on the position, then at around 7.30 am on 17th April the first heavy (21cm) shell exploded in the centre of von Tschurtschenthaler's position and was immediately followed by many more. The bombardment increased in intensity with heavy grenades and shrapnel of all calibres. General Henry Shrapnel is the name of the inventor of that diabolical

Museo della Grande Guerra, Rovereto

Michael Wachtler

Left: The miseries of captivity during the battles for the Col di Lana. Two Austrian POWs, one very young, the other much older wolf down their food. Right: An Austrian combat patrol has captured an enemy soldier. Dressed in winter gear they proudly show off their victim.

cast-iron shell designed to explode before impact, producing a shower of lead balls and fragments, wreaking havoc over an area of 200 metres' diameter.

The attack continued all day long, heavy mortars exploded close to the Austrian caverns. Soldiers retreated to their shelters with guns and hand grenades at the ready to ward off a potential infantry attack and the exposed posts were reduced to minimum manning. Granades and shells exploded in front of the entrance to the large cavern in which the men had taken refuge, blocking their exit with boulders and fallen material. Even though the rubble was quickly cleared the resulting influx of cordite fumes from succeeding explosions soon made breathing for the 100 men within the cavern almost impossible and demanded its partial clearance because of occupants losing consciousness through lack of oxygen. Men were employed to waft large blankets to fan in fresh air. The barrage continued all afternoon and evening until just past 9 pm when the firing

ceased. The fire trenches had all been destroyed, the access points to the position were for the most part buried and von Tschurtschenthaler gave the order for engineers to repair the damage to afford some defence during the expected forthcoming infantry attack. The field telephone line had been cut all day and any communication to the rear had been impossible during the barrage. The line was restored at 10 pm and von Tschurtschenthaler reported the events of the day to the battalion commander, reiterating his request – sent earlier with some lightly wounded soldiers and subsequently by messenger - for reinforcements and help with rebuilding the position. Italians were sighted crawling forward.

The positions were immediately manned, the battalion commander informed, who put the sector artillery on standby and von Tschurtschenthaler moved inside the cavern with the telephone. The night was pitch dark. Lieutenant Gelasio Caetani waited tensely, the five minutes seemed an

Michael Wachtler

Above left: A shell hits the peak of the Lagazuoi. Above right: An Austrian gun inside a cavern. Right: As the war went on the huts became increasingly cosy and more homely.

Günther Obwegs, Gottfried Leitgeb

eternity. At 11.35 the mountain trembled, as if it were to collapse in on itself amid a deafening crash, followed by concussion from the blast and the racket of rocks and boulders falling down the mountainside. Then came the climax as the drumfire started again. The moans and cries for help of the badly wounded and hideously disfigured men rose above the hellish din, men who had been catapulted through the air and were lying helpless among the rubble or in the Seif gorge.

Von Tschurtschenthaler and some 60 survivors were once again trapped inside the cavern. Within five minutes the Italians had stormed the peak and overcame what little resistance could be offered by the stunned survivors. In the cavern Anton von Tschurtschenthaler restored calm, had the entrance to the tunnel manned and gave the order to hold out as long as possible. However, with the Italians at a tunnel

entrance, what if they threw hand grenades inside and caused a bloodbath among the remaining survivors? Outside over 100 of their comrades lay dead. Once again the cavern began to fill with cordite fumes and the first men were succumbing. The first candles went out. Minute by minute the situation became more and more critical. The men were faced with three choices: to break out and be killed, to stay inside and suffocate, or to surrender and become prisoners.

They were left with no choice but to surrender. Von Tschurtschenthaler sent his senior non-commissioned officer, Oberjäger Galvanini to parley with Don Gelasio Caetani. Shortly thereafter the cavern garrison, after bidding each other farewell, surrendered to the Italian infantry. Would they ever meet again? Who could tell. After a silent and firm handshake the survivors climbed in the direction of the mountain summit amid

C. Balelli, Bibl. Naz. Macerata

Loris Lancedelli, A. Piersanti

Left: Italian soldiers observe the Austrian positions on the Lagazuoi from the Cima Gallina. Soldiers are protected behind an abundance of jute sacks filled with gravel. Right: Hundreds of Alpini soldiers labour uphill, hauling a cannon in the Cinque Torri area.

horrific devastation. Their weapons were thrown down the mountain. A deep crater opened before them, in which over a hundred men had been buried and killed in seconds. With tears in their eyes they approached the Italian commander with the request that he should take care of the badly wounded men left behind in the cavern. Over a hundred men were taken prisoner. Over the following days Italian troops still found men beneath the rubble, desperately waiting for help under rocks and beams in excruciating pain. Many were dead, others grateful to the enemy for being rescued at the last minute. That was the day when the Col di Lana, the 'Bloody Mountain' was blown up by the Italian troops.

18,000 soldiers on both the Austrian and Italian sides died or were wounded on the Col di Lana. Afterwards the Austrian field marshal Ludwig Goiginger could only ask with resignation "Who deserves more ad-

miration in these battles, the Italians who, in spite of such dreadful losses continued to attack the pernicious mountain over and over, or the small number of defenders who held out in this hell and heroically repulsed all those attacks?"

The Lagazuoi is blasted into the sky

On the Lagazuoi alone the Austrians made four attempts and the Italians one to achieve their aims by means of massive explosions. As a result of the third blasting by the Austrians on 22nd May 1917 some 100,000 cubic metres of rock thundered to valley. The gains were minimal. A rock face 200 metres high and 136 metres wide was blown away and crashed into the cirque beneath, though it proved insufficient to dislodge the enemy. Less than a month later the Italians made their retaliatory strike.

The blasting of the Lagazuoi was merely a response to the same technique employed by the Italians a year earlier on the Col di Lana (though the first mine – the 'New Year's Day explosion' was detonated on the Lagazuoi by the Austrians on 1st January 1916 using 'only' 300 kg of dynamite beneath an Italian observation post). Mountains together with their occupants were simply blown away.

A second 2,656 metre-high bastion of rock towers beside the Lagazuoi: the Punta di Bòis. During the war the Italians dubbed it Castelletto because it resembled a castle, while the Austrians had their own name for it: Schreckenstein, i.e., 'rock of horrors'. A further detail contributed to ensuring that this Cima di Bòis went down in history, namely the group of future famous personalities which originated from the core for-

Michael Wachtler

The blasting of the Punta di Bòis on 11th July 1916 with an entry by Captain Carl von Raschin. The authenticity of the picture is disputed, with critics arguing that there could never have been so much light at 3.30 am. On the other hand nobody can explain how the photograph could have been retouched.

mation of the Kaiserjäger soldiers who were defending this mountain. They included the famous author, film star and director Luis Trenker, whose two books Fort Rocca Alta and Mountains in Flames, were based on his wartime experiences, the latter forming the basis of a film; Hans Schneeberger, cinematographer; Hubert Mumelter, author; and Carl von Raschin, author. Here too, time and again the Italians stormed the rock and were easily repulsed, for the Austrian position had been so fortified as to be unassailable.

The Italians began to change their tactics. At the beginning of 1916 Colonel Giuseppe Tarditi, revered for his organisational abilities, gave the order to excavate a 400 metre-long gallery beneath the mountain. The Punta di Bòis was ready to be blown up on 11th July 1916 in the presence of the King, Vittorio Emanuele III; the supreme commander of the Italian forces, General Cadorna; and other high-ranking dignitaries, all of whom were watching from a safe vantage point near the Cinque Torri. 37,000 kg of explosives - solidified nitro-glycerine - were to be detonated.

Perhaps Hans Schneeberger described best the general mood during the blast: "Agitated thoughts: The detonation...so soon... The blast and the end. My chest is under pressure...tighter and tighter...I can hardly breathe anymore. The air is murky, thick with dust and full of the stench of sulphur. I'm still reeling, I stagger up and outside. The sky has disappeared. A cloud envelops everything: the mountain and huts, sky and stars." Some 30 Austrians died, 20 of them because they had disobeyed orders and were sleeping in a hut in the middle of the saddle. This explosion, like others, had no significant effect on the outcome of the war. The Italians advanced a little, then the old stalemate resumed.

British officers observe enemy positions on the Asiago plateau.

Allied troops in the Alps

At the Rome conference in January 1917 the British prime minister, Lloyd George, promised Italy assistance with British and French heavy artillery should the need arise. Following a massive combined Austro-German attack in the upper Isonzo valley at Caporetto on 24th October, 1917 with poison gas and heavy bombardment, the broken Italian forces were driven back 40 miles west as far as the River Piave, leaving the government no alternative but to plead with the Allies for help. By 27th October French advance parties had arrived. An initial British force, consisting of the XIV Corps under the command of the Earl of Cavan, with the 23rd and 41st Divisions was despatched and began to arrive on 11th November 1917.

On the 13th Sir Herbert Plumer, dubbed the 'Soldiers' General', arrived and assumed command of the British forces in Italy. These troops were followed by the 5th, 7th and 48th Divisions. In spite of his appearance (a 'Colonel Blimp' image -

smart to a fault, white hair, white moustache, pot-belly, strict disciplinarian) belied the fact that Plumer was one of the best-performing and best-regarded officers and one of the most brilliant strategists on the Allied side.

Plumer never got on with Commander-in-Chief Haig (as an examiner he once gave Haig low marks!) but always remained loyal to him despite personal differences. It was Plumer's abilities which induced Haig to put him in command of the British forces in Italy, ordering him to leave the Western Front for Italy on 9th November 1917. Obviously

First commander of the British troops in Italy: Sir Herbert Plumer.

51

the Allies were unwilling to see Italy collapse. By 16th November the Austro-German offensive had ground to a halt (for the Germans this offensive had been tactical rather than strategic, to keep Austria-

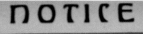

ΠΟΤΙϹΕ

Estaminets are closed to British soldiers exc
during the following hours :

12 noon to 2 p. m.
6 p. m. to 8 p. m.

Estaminets must be clear of troops by 8 p.

The sale of light wine and beer only is permi
spirits are strictly forbidden. Soldiers are not
served in back rooms.

Gambling of all sorts is forbidden.

Estaminet proprietors who serve troops
unauthorised hours, or whose Estaminets are
perly conducted, will have their premises p
of bounds.

30 December 1917.

B Generale Addetto
L. PICCIONE

W. WESTERN M
D. A. G.

Rules of behaviour for British soldiers on the southern front.

British positions on the Asiago plateau. The main body of the British forces was concentrated in this area.

Hungary in the war, not to occupy Northern Italy). In just three weeks 10,000 Italians had died and 30,000 were wounded, while 265,000 were taken prisoner. Arduously a new line of defence had to be constructed and the Italian forces needed to be reorganised. The unfortunate General Luigi Cadorna was dismissed and the task fell to Armando Diaz.

The British forces were concentrated mainly in the Piave Valley as far as the Montello hills, and on the Asiago Plateau, a rocky cluster of peaks and ridges to the

north of Vicenza, while the French expeditionary force of the 10th Army Division under the command of General Duchêne was stationed to the west of Verona at the southern end of Lake Garda in order to repulse a rumoured Austrian offensive from the north through the Adige Valley. They regarded it as a good omen that Napoleon's army had defeated the Austrians there in 1809.

The Americans entered the war on 6th April 1917 as an 'Associated Nation' of the Allies. One infantry regiment, the 332nd, served in Italy, along with several supply and medical units. In addition, a number of American Red Cross (ARC) and YMCA personnel provided care and comforts to the Italian Army, and later to the 332nd Infantry, its support units and the US Military Mission. A number of US trainee pilots were sent to Italy under the inspiring leadership of Fiorello La Guardia, at that time a lawyer and recently-elected Congressman for the 14th District of New York. In addition, significant numbers of immigrants returned to Italy as reservists or volunteers for the Italian Army. However, given that America did not declare war on Austria-Hungary until 7th December 1917, initially they had to keep out of the conflict.

The celebrated badly wounded Ernest Hemingway

One American Red Cross volunteer was later to become famous: the eighteen year-old Ernest Hemingway. He arrived from Paris and was at first stationed at Schio to collect the wounded in Fiat truck. Soon afterwards the fiercest battles began on the Piave following the defeat at Caporetto. There Captain James Gamble needed somebody to cycle directly to the front twice daily to hand out chocolate and cigarettes. Medical Officer Hemingway volunteered for the task. On 8th July 1918 he rode past a trench near the village of Fossalta to distribute food when an Austrian mortar bomb fired from a 420 launcher exploded right beside him. He later described the following months in his 1929 cult novel 'A Farewell to Arms'.

He became the first badly wounded American of the First World War and was correspondingly celebrated. One Italian soldier died immediately, another had both his legs blown off. Once he had regained consciousness Hemingway, badly wounded, helped the man to the first aid station. Over two hundred splinters of shrapnel had become embedded in Hemingway's legs. Had he been less robust and strong

Ernest Hemmingway, later to become famous as an American author and winner of the Nobel Prize for literature, shown here before seeing active service on the Italian front, then badly wounded in hospital.

he would hardly have survived. Instead he was given the highest military honours – the Italian government even bestowed the silver medal for bravery upon him. He ended up in a military hospital in Milan from where, after a long convalescence leave, he sailed on the boat 'Giuseppe Verde' to America as a war hero.

British forces in Italy

At the time the front stretched from the Swiss border to the Adriatic, over 180 kilometres as the crow flies. At peak in Jan-

French helpers on the Italian Front.

A British observation post near Asiago.

uary 1918 there were almost 114,000 British troops in Italy with 26,000 horses. Their contribution to the outcome of the war was to a large extent underestimated, for this 'Forgotten Front' contained an essential seed of the overall victory. The Italian army was completely demoralised and fragmented, now it was receiving support, the front line became more stable. German troops had only been 'on loan' to the Austrians and now they were needed on the Western Front. With their departure the situation became less tense. Haig ordered Plumer back to France and he departed with the 5th and 41st Divisions in February 1918.

Frederick Rudolf Lambart, 10th Earl of Cavan took over from him. Together with the XIV Corps he had achieved recognition on the Western Front as one of the most successful unit commanders. Later in 1918 he was even given command of the 10th Italian Army which played a decisive part in the victory of the battle of Vittorio Veneto, the final battle of the war in Italy, after which the Austrian army, demoralised with virtually non-existent supplies and equipment, virtually disintegrated and ceased to function as an effective fighting force. The victory heralded the end to hostilities on the Western Front.

At the beginning the Allied troops were faced with problems in unloading vast numbers of men, vehicles and horses at small country railway stations. The situation was made worse by a lack of interpreters. Each battalion was supposed to be assigned one Italian liaison officer fluent in English and several interpreters, though the reality turned out differently. Norman Gladden, a soldier with the 11th Northumberland Fusiliers noted that the British were sent, among other things, to set an example:

54

British troops established their camp in the area of Granezza.

British troops observe positions on the Asiago plateau.

Austrian soldiers are led away by their British captors.

After the recall of Plumer to France the supreme command of the British Forces in Italy passed to Frederick Rudolf Lambart, Earl of Cavan. British camp on the Asiago plateau.

"The local population, and newspaper reporters from across Italy, were suitably impressed by the long columns of Allied soldiers; smart, disciplined, healthy, cheerful and vigorous. They were in sharp contrast to stragglers from Caporetto slowly making their way westwards. These Sbanditi were shepherded into assembly areas well away from the operational zone; quiet places where shattered units could rally, and exhausted and demoralised men recover in body and soul. But the Italian nation rallied after the disaster at Caporetto; and propaganda posters appeared everywhere, exhorting everyone to fight and support the nation in its time of danger."

The beginning of the end

During 1918 the Italians were encouraged by the fact that the enemy's morale was even worse than their own and that Austria-Hungary was politically on the point of disintegration. The increasing importance of America was also a morale-booster among Italians.

To capitalise on the low morale in the Austrian army a systematic propaganda campaign was launched with the help of captured Czechs, Slovaks, Slavs and others, directed at the Empire's disaffected ethnic minorities. At the same time, once it had become clear that the German offensive of April 1918 had not produced a decisive outcome, General Ludendorff pressurised the Austrians into launching a strong offensive across the Piave River in the vicinity of several major Italian cities (Padova, Verona). The purpose was to relieve pressure on the German armies on the Western Front. The Germans even feared that Italian troops could be sent to France to reinforce the Allies. A psychological motive was to follow up the spectacular success of the 'Wonder of Caporetto' and knock Italy out of the war altogether.

Austria-Hungary launched what was to be their final offensive on Italian soil during World War One between 15th and 22nd June 1918. The objective was to cross the Piave River and, via the mountain plateau of Asiago, to breach the Allied resistance in a pincer movement, then form an operations centre at Treviso, after which Allied resistance was expected to collapse. With the Austrian army lacking supplies, back-up forces, all aggravated by heavy rain

War material abandoned by the Austrians after the Battle of the Piave River from 15th to 22nd June, 1918.

which flooded the river - in places 800 yards wide and fast-flowing - the outcome of the offensive was disastrous. There was a wave of desertions and Field Marshal von Hoetzendorff was removed as commander.

The Austrian Empire was subsequently doomed and the army, severely weakened, unlikely to withstand the next Allied counter attack which came four months later in the same sector of the River Piave. On 14th June 1918 the Austro-Hungarian troops were told that a decisive battle lay ahead which would procure them eternal glory, honour and above all, good food and peace. Next day, 15th June the attack began at 3 a.m. with a massive poison gas cannonade in the Val Lagarina, actually the Adige Valley to the south of Trento. To quote G. M. Trevelyan:

"The offensive was launched with equal fury along an unbroken line of attack stretching from the Asiago front opposite the British, right round by Grappa, the Montello, and the course of the Piave down to the sea. At dawn on June 15th it began along this great stretch of ground with a bombardment of terrible efficiency. "Some of the British officers told me they had never seen better shooting or a hotter barrage in France. The result was that early that morning the Austrians carried with little resistance almost the whole front line

The road into captivity: the Austrian Empire lost 100,000 men in this offensive.

of the Allies from Asiago to the marshes at the Piave mouth."

However, the initial success was to prove short-lived. The Austrians were driven back into their own territory with terrible losses, and by 20th June it had become obvious that the Piave offensive had failed, for 12,000 prisoners had been taken and large quantities of material had fallen into Allied hands. Torrential rain had swollen

The original telegram announcing the armistice on the southern front, sent to Major V. F. Eberle, Royal Engineers, received on 4th November 1918 at 2am.

the river. Italy was jubilant when the offensive collapsed completely on 23rd June. The disgrace of Caporetto was forgotten, Italy could once again raise her head proudly. Instinctively people felt that a turning point had come, not just on the River Piave but in the course of the war in general. Against all expectations it seemed as if, once they were fighting for the survival of their own people and defending their own territory, Italians had become a united and fierce enemy. Railway lines were improved and the armaments industry was once again able to provide large quantities of supplies.

The Austro-Hungarian army had lost 64,000 men with many more taken prisoner, and there were tumultuous scenes in the Hungarian parliament when the Minister of Defence, M. Wekerle, was

forced to admit that most of the dead were Hungarians used as cannon fodder. This sealed the destiny of the war. Austrian resistance lingered on for another four months until the beginning of November 1918. Nevertheless losses among Allied forces during the week from 15th to 23rd June 1918 were also considerable: the Italians lost 85,000 men, against 64,000 Austrians.

During the entire 1917-18 Italian campaign British losses amounted to 90 officers and 1,200 other ranks (in addition to 759 who died of disease or injury). 4,700 men were wounded and 50,000 reported sick at some point, of which 11,500 had influenza. The French lost 592 soldiers. As an indication as to the modern nature of the campaign, British troops shot down 386 enemy aircraft, 27 balloons, against British losses of 47 aircraft.

Italian soldiers enter Trento.

Crossing the Cordevole on 2nd November 1918.

Italian troops in Meran.

The German-speaking town of Meran after being occupied by Italian troops. Initially life had to go on as usual, people had to get used to the new circumstances.

Foto Waldmüller, archive Helmut Rainer (3)

Sweethearts and whores

There is nothing like war to make men inconsiderate and turn them into animals. Sex and whoring were one of the main causes of the deplorable conditions which prevailed in the universally revered Austro-Hungarian army. People took venereal diseases in their stride and they were rarely mentioned. Not even when, alone in the Austro-Hungarian army, 1,275,885 persons were officially infected, almost as many as those suffering from the typical scourges of war, typhoid, malaria, dysentery and tuberculosis together. These diseases may have caused more fatalities, but the 'Dance of the Gonococci', the bacterium causing gonorrhoea and the spirochaetes responsible for syphilis caused mass but hushed-up epidemics. As early as 24th October 1915 the Austrian imperial command on the south-western front issued a 'Prostitution Regulation'

which could hardly have been more urgent: "Soldiers! The battle man against man has cost some of you your lives, while others have been wounded or disabled. ... But what about the fight between man and wench?" It continued: "With smiles on their faces women and girls will sap your strength and health."

At that point the authorities investigated the causes. It was revealed that the Innsbruck military command accounted for 13.4 percent of persons infected with sexually transmitted diseases. This resulted in girls as young as fifteen having to be treated. Among 1,000 girls infected, 91 were aged under 18, almost ten percent. Great efforts went into informing soldiers, encouraging them to use condoms and to look after their bodies. The high command was helplessly ambivalent, unable to decide whether or not to punish infected sol-

A unique photographic document. At first this girl from the Cortina area at work in the fields looks coyly towards the Italian soldiers.

diers. If draconian punishments were meted out soldiers would deny being infected and spread their diseases still further. On the other hand, dismissing venereal disease infections as mere peccadilloes would open the floodgates.

Compared with other warring nations the condition and fighting effectiveness of the imperial army was impaired to a greater extent. This was partly as a result of a tradition of sexual freedom bordering on promiscuity throughout the Austrian Empire which had carried on tacitly for decades. Even before the war sexually transmitted diseases accounted for "17 to 31 percent of all illnesses" among members of the Austrian armed forces. Once war had broken out the incidence of VD increased further to the point where the high command feared that it could seriously impair the war effort. They felt forced to revert to drastic measures to halt the epidemic and adopted means which today might strike us as bizarre.

Field brothels as tactical institution

In typical 'Old Austrian' style so-called legalised 'field brothels' were set up. Special regulations were introduced "Concerning the setting-up, organisation, running, as well as the military supervision, subordination and administration of mobile field and reserve brothels." This publication was distributed among all positions southward to the Isonzo, the Dolomites and Trento. This was followed by a plethora of articles in flawless legalese:

"1. Designation. The field and reserve brothels constitute in integrated element of the army in the field. They will be named according to their divisions as Field Brothel No..., or Reserve Brothel No.... .

2. Purpose: Their purpose is the sexual relief of officers and other ranks...

3. ...medical institutions staffed with Red Cross nurses will not be granted field brothels, given that the members of the armed

Massimo Turkheimer, Foto Edoardo Turkheimer (3)

The officer tries first of all to curry favour with the girl and she quickly succumbs to his advances.

An Italian propaganda postcard. Bewitching women create the impression that it is sweet to die for the fatherland.

forces recovering there are to a certain extent able to provide themselves with right or left-handed serving female persons... ."

Nurses and female orderlies as whores. They were expected by law to indulge the lusts of the soldiers, whether they liked it or not.

All kinds of suggestions were considered to get a grip on the sexual needs of the proud army, but with a ridiculousness which could all have come straight from a comedy play were it not for the tragic explosive nature of the problem concealed in all sorts of nuances. Article 5 even regulated the "Rank and command structures. The headship of the field brothel institutions is incumbent on the head of the field brothel system." The legislator even worked out a hierarchy and rules for promotion. Girls became mere playthings of the soldiers. They were expected to relinquish their morals, raise the level of adrenalin and produce benefits which could help with the war efforts. "The female crews are divided into three groups: a) Officers' girls, b) Other ranks' whores 1st

class and c) Other ranks' whores 2nd class. The latter bear the designation 'trench women'. There can be no advancement from the categories b or c." So there were no chances of promotion! The article stipulating work clothing is even more bizarre, so ridiculous that the legislation was destined to failure. "The female personnel will wear standardised military-grey ('hecht-grau') field uniforms of the existing type worn by Red Cross nurses ... the underwear will be as follows: normal underwear suitable for extended wear ... While carrying out their duty they may take off their uniforms completely or partially. While doing so they must take care of their clothing." The law regulates all aspects meticulously: the uniforms may be taken off while performing the sexual act but must be kept in a constantly clean condition.

Sin, sex and shame

The constant inhuman stress, not knowing if one would survive the next day, produced some rather strange and bizarre results.

"Love" is the caption, the village in the background is Cortina. In spite of this, in the end there were scenes of fraternising between village girls and the foreign (Italian) occupants which were condemned by the older village folk.

Though not only on one's own side. The war developed into a sink of iniquity nonpareil. From Radersdorf in Styria an Italian prisoner of war wrote to Castel San Giovanni, Piacenza: "I'm in the house of a woman..., whose man is on the front. She is completely besotted with be. I have nothing to complain about..."

Even cheating was regarded as a just means of warfare, given that men supposed with good reason that the same conditions also prevailed in Italy: "... seeing that we have to pleasure women whose husbands are prisoners in Italy; and that which we are doing the others are doing exactly the same with our women." And he probably was not very wrong either.

Change of scene to Cortina d'Ampezzo. Cortina, which was abandoned without a fight by the Austrians in order to shorten the front could be seen as a perfect case in point to illustrate sexual behaviour during the First World War. The parish archives entry of 31st December 1916 is a sort of general résumé of the situation in this capital town of the Dolomites (around 6,000 inhabitants): "Year 1916. Marriages: none. Deaths: 76. Births: 47. Of which in wedlock: 21, out of wedlock: 26, among which there were 10 married women whose husbands have been in action on the front for over a year!! We should not pause to describe the worse cases of fornication, there were far too many in number!."

A message, the consequences of which have until now been insufficiently recognised. The majority of children born in Cortina had Italian fathers (at the time Cortina was still predominantly Ladin). The locum tenens of the church at Cortina Don Cristoforo Rizzardi censured the - as he saw it - dissolute behaviour of these women and during Mass gave his flock a good and proper reading from Leviticus. Maria Menardi who was an assiduous diary write noted down the essence of his sermon: "He ad-

An Austrian postcard from the First World War. When morale was at its deepest womanhood became elevated to a pure, immaculate object of desire. Right: A picture of careless intimacy. A soldier takes two girls on a rowing jaunt on the Pordoi-Joch pass. The incidence of sexually transmitted diseases among soldiers was shockingly high. The authorities were too ashamed to publish the figures.

monished the youth always to comport themselves decently and to avoid bad company, but he addressed the married women even more forcefully, reminding them of their duties towards their husbands on the front and to their children ...”

The deployment of women in military and field hospitals degenerated into a veritable marriage market. Soon the press and literature began to ridicule the picture of these erotic flirtations. And even the celebrated author Ernest Hemingway, later to become a Nobel Prize winner for literature, became the centre of attention in hospital because of a love affair. He was badly wounded while serving as a medical orderly in the Italian army on the south-western front and while recovering in hospital he fell helplessly in love with an American nurse. Women slipped into cliché roles and were at one time ‘angels’, then ‘sex objects’ though not only men but also women contributed their share. Many in the upper echelons of the military command were literally “mobbed by dubious females in fairy-like dress” who were “helplessly in love” with the officers. The nurses on the other hand could afford to be choosy. It was regarded as noble to give first aid to the wounded and badly wounded, while the treatment of the many

sexually transmitted diseases was the least of their priorities.

The sexual drive of both men and women developed into a war within a war in other ways as well. The flirtatious behaviour between the female population and prisoners was observed Argus-eyed by the authorities, and many women encouraged the men’s attentions. Too many men were on the front and too many people, men and girls, prisoners, warriors, women and lonely hearts fell into each others arms. And this gave rise to crises which, quite apart from the normal horrors of war often led into the abysses of human existence.

An Italian prisoner of war held in the Katzenau camp near Linz wrote to his unfaithful wife: “Your misdeeds are so many that there is little point in listing them. You simply give yourself to the first man who lands between your legs, and with such ease, not out of love but because a perverse sexual drive. You have the nerve to call it ‘enthusiasm’. ... You have fallen into the dirt, completely. There are few women who are worth loving, but those who leave their husbands because of an excess of ‘enthusiasm’ and then besmirch his name even further through their behaviour to climb to the final rung of prostitution, are definitely not

A fire destroyed the hamlet of Campo near Cortina on 4th October 1916. Eleven families lost their homes and all their possessions. It gradually transpired that the reason for the disaster was the unrequited love of an Italian officer for a pretty girl from Campo.

among them. Wife, calamity, disaster. Woman, cat, heretic."

The sufferings of the cuckolded

Another soldier held prisoner at Bruck an der Mur in Styria wrote with even more powerful eloquence to his wife at Cervignano (Friuli): "Wife? I still call you that purely out of politeness, otherwise I would have to call you a hussy. How could you have done this to me with your letter, to me, this innocent victim and leave me to die with it. .... You are a whore, yes, a prostitute. ... Carry on indulging yourself as far as I'm concerned, and do whatever seems right to you. A thousand kisses from your beloved husband N. and think of all those repulsive things you have done to your unfortunate husband."

And how did women endure this world of the biblical Sodom and Gomorrah? They saw the errors and sins of their neighbours. They reassured their husbands that they were among the few not to have succumbed to harlotry – it was always the neighbour's wife: "How many hapless men will eventually return home to find not two or three, but suddenly four or five children. I wouldn't want to be in their shoes, for almost all married women, even

the reasonably decent ones have fallen into prostitution. I have only one love in this life and that is you, for if I really was such a tart I would never write to you...."

Not write anymore to one's own spouse. How often was that the case and how often did people have to lie? A woman wrote these lines of fidelity to Ufa in Russia, squealing on her husband's younger sister: "I peeped behind a fence and saw with my own eyes two people wrapped together. I have to tell you, P. that one of them was your little sister and the other was the old, revolting broom maker, the one with the turned-up moustache. P., I just can't believe it, to catch your sister with this dreadful old man in the middle of a field going at it worse than dogs do."

Never were so many sins committed than during the war. Everywhere. For example in Vienna where abortion was harshly punished the number of abortions rose dramatically, from just 1.4 per thousand births in 1913 to 4 in 1915, while in 1916 the number increased to 5.3. It came to devastating estrangements. Women became estranged from their husbands because they had committed adultery, while there were likewise soldiers who preferred active service on the front to life at home.

The case of Cesare Battisti

The sentenced had been passed even before his trial. As soon as the news arrived that the traitor had been caught the executioner from Vienna, Josef Lang, set out on the train to Trento. The trial was a farce. Sentence was passed at 4.30 pm on 12th July 1916 and less than three hours later the man from Trento Dr. Cesare Battisti, 2nd lieutenant in the Italian Alpine Corps and former Austrian member of parliament in Vienna, was dead. He had been captured the day before fighting against the Austrians in the mountains behind Rovereto and immediately identified as an Austrian. The inhuman treatment he suffered and the form of his death turned him into a martyr. Today throughout Italy roads and squares are named after him. The imperial Austrian legislature had done everything it could to humiliate him. He was refused anything which could have made his fate more bearable. His request to be shot – a more honourable death, after all he had been caught in uniform - was refused and he was forced to face the execution of death by hanging, in reality a form of slow strangulation. He was not allowed to die in his Italian uniform and was required to pay 39 crowns for a chequered suit which was far too big for him. Battisti became a symbol of the decadent Austrian monarchy and laid bare the double standards which applied in that multiethnic state. He was born in 1875 in Trento as son of a well-to-do family of shopkeepers, studied law and philosophy at Florence, Graz, Vienna and Turin. He soon became involved in campaigning for an improved status of the Italian ethnic group within the Austrian Empire, and especially his home region, Trentino. Trentino was underdeveloped, a part of the German Tyrol but with only 300,000 inhabitants in a region with 600,000 ethnic Germans. They had no university of their own. National pressure was mounting to eradicate Italian. There was even a movement to Germanise Italian place names in Trentino. Cesare Battisti was opposed this and even went as far as to demand the frontier between Austria and Italy to be established at Salurn, the present-day border between Trentino and South Tyrol (not at the Brenner Pass, where it is today). He founded newspapers, became a book publisher, was elected to the Tyrolean regional parliament and became an MP in the Viennese parliament as representative of the Socialist Party.

Then came World War One. True to his principles, together with his wife and children he moved to Italy and joined the Italian army, requesting to be posted to the front line. In the meantime men from Trentino who were loyal to Austria were sacrificed as cannon fodder on the Russian front in Galicia (an old Austrian province now divided between Poland and Ukraine). 8,000 'Trentini' Kaiserjäger died there, over 22%, the highest percentage among all Austrian regions. 75,000 Trentini were forcibly evacuated and accommodated in camps unfit for human beings in Bohemia, Upper Austria, especially the camp at Katzenau near Linz. The dreaded 'wooden shanty towns' were built hurriedly at the outbreak of war at Mitterndorf, Pottendorf and Braunau. Anybody who finished up there could only fear the worst. Disease caused by the unsanitary conditions, hunger, overcrowding and privation in general resulted in untold deaths among refugees. One of the most unpleasant episodes of the Austro-Hungarian empire reached its climax with the case of Cesare Battisti as its figurehead and martyr. His death on the gallows did more damage to the Austrian war effort than most occurrences in battle. Shortly before his death he wrote to his fifteen year-old son who was determined to join the war: "The war is turning our Trentino into wasteland and a graveyard. You young ones must prepare to rebuild it."

One of the most deeply symbolic photographs from the First World War which the Austrian journalist Karl Kraus immortalised with an enthralling caption:

"Above all it is the (countenance) of the hangman. Of the Viennese hangman on this postcard which shows the dead Battisti, the hangman standing there like a triumphant stuffed dummy, his paws above the dead man's head expressing satisfied smugness. Grinning faces of civilians and others whose last possession is privilege, crowd around the corpse doing whatever they can to get onto the postcard."

Cesare Battisti was captured by Austrian troops on Monte Corno to the east of Rovereto. Cesare Battisti, Trentino member of the Imperial Parliament in Vienna marches majestically to his court martial. After a degrading trial he was found guilty of treason and hanged like a criminal on 12th July 1916. He was fighting for the border to be established at Salurn.

67

Museo della Guerra Bianca, Temù

Little brother, don't be sad!

Clelia Calvi from Piazza Brembana bore four sons. They grew up, and then the war began. The first to die was Attilio Calvi on the Adamello. He earned the bronze medal for bravery, then the silver then, after he had fallen, again the silver medal, the one with a black loop awarded posthumously. He fell badly wounded on the Passo Fargorida. The next to fall was the 22 year-old Santino, hit by a fatal bullet from an Austrian Schwarzlose machine gun on 10th June 1916. Then the 18 year-old Giannino was given his uniform. After fighting numerous heroic battles he died from a deadly attack of influenza. Clelia's fourth and last remaining son Natale Calvi survived the war. He fell to his death in 1920 while attempting to scale the north face of the Adamello by himself. The mother, Clelia Calvi was left alone. Such stories can only be understood in depth by disregarding nationalism. Peoples' souls should speak out. The Calvi brothers and Sepp Innerkofler fought for different countries but for the same ideal. May the death of Attilo Calvi (picture above) and that of Sepp Innerkofler (picture opposite page) awaken a feeling of compassion for all.

68

Gottfried Inneerkofler

In 1918 a group of friends climbed up to the summit of the Paternkofel to retrieve his body, which they lowered down the rock face in a coffin.

Sepp Innerkofler-mountain guide

Sepp Innerkofler became a symbolic figure of enormous importance among the Austro-Hungarian mountain troops. He was already 50 when he volunteered to fight on the Dolomite with his 19 year-old son Gottfried. He was regarded as one of the last great pioneers, with incomparable knowledge of the area and terrain who had chalked up tens of first ascents. By 3rd July 1915 he had already been decorated and promoted to NCO. On that day he had been sent with a small team on a night mission to take the Paternkofel in the Sexten Dolomites. He arrived close beneath the summit when an Alpino soldier looked down onto the ledge beneath him and was shocked to discover Sepp Innerkofler. There are various accounts of his death, but it is almost certain that he had been noticed at first light by a soldier who fought him in hand-to-hand contact on a narrow ledge. When the Italian managed to disengage himself for a moment he picked up a rock and smashed it into Innerkofler's face, causing him to plummet to his death.

Risking their lives, two Italian soldiers, Loschi and Vesello climbed down to the place where Sepp Innerkofler's body had landed and recognised him as the most famous mountain guide of his age. They tied the lifeless body with rope and hauled him up to the summit ridge where he was buried with due reverence. A simple cross tied with Innerkofler's climbing rope inscribed 'Sepp Innerkofler – Guida' (mountain guide) marked his grave.

The girl soldier Viktoria Savs

It became unavoidable in this long struggle for women to begin playing a role on the front. Viktoria Savs, the sixteen-year-old daughter of Peter Savs was determined to accompany her father to the front. He had been wounded fighting the Russians but, having recovered, volunteered to join the Landsturm, the equivalent of a territorial army for the defence of the homeland. He tried to dissuade Viktoria, explained the dangers, arguing that there was not a woman anywhere who could withstand service in the forward positions armed with a rifle. To no avail. Viktoria wrote personally to Archduke Eugen asking for exceptional permission. Nobody believed it possible, but she was accepted.

Father and daughter Savs left for the Dolomite front in June 1915. The girl volunteered for everything. In April 1917 she escorted a dozen Italian prisoners to her troops under heavy artillery fire. The young soldier 'Viktor' Savs was greatly admired for 'his' courage and spirit of comradeship.

Then on 27th May 1917 Viktoria volunteered to carry a message. She climbed with agility among the rocks until there was a dreadful crash

Viktoria Savs

and bang as a shell thundered overhead and exploded against the rock face, loosening a massive rock. Viktoria Savs felt a terrible pain and noticed that she could no longer move her right foot. Her lower leg below the knee was only hanging on a few sinews. Then she lost consciousness. When she came to she still had enough strength to take her penknife from her anorak and tried to cut off her foot. Help finally arrived and she was given first aid.

She was unable to remember any of these occurrences when she awoke in a primitive field hospital at Sillian, surrounded by astonished men. The truth about her identity had been uncovered: the courageous soldier Viktor Savs was in reality a girl. She looked down and saw that, where her right leg had once been, there was now only a pathetically bandaged stump. She was honoured with the Silver Medal first class for bravery. Gradually her comrades began to find out who she really was and spoke of her reverently as the 'girl hero of the Drei Zinnen'. In the chaos and confusion of the post war years she reached Salzburg as a stateless person. Viktoria Savs had to scrape to get by, with hunger as her constant companion and without disability benefits. She was officially stateless and had to bear her misfortune until one day in 1935 she saw the man walking past in a sumptuous uniform to whom she had once written when she was sixteen: Archduke Eugen. She limped and hesitated, then plucked up courage and approached the old duke in a field marshal's uniform as he strode past. She asked him humbly in her abject hardship for nothing more than to be accepted as a citizen of the country for which she had been willing to lay down her life.

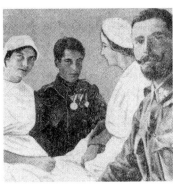

Viktoria Savs during the winter of 1916 on a perilous message run. Only a few officers knew the true identity of the 'volunteer soldier Viktor' who was serving in the same unit as 'his' father. Finally in the field hospital her secret was revealed and it emerged that her real name was Viktoria. Above, centre: Her father (in the foreground) consoles the courageous girl. When Viktoria Savs died in 1979 few people still remembered the 'girl hero of the Drei Zinnen' with her decorations and the medals she earned for bravery.

Ergeben in den Willen Gottes geben wir bekannt, daß meine liebe Schwiegermutter und Schwester, Frau

VIKTORIA SAVS
„Das Heldenmädchen von den 3 Zinnen"
Trägerin der großen Silbernen Tapferkeitsmedaille
und mehrerer Kriegsauszeichnungen (1914–1918)
Mitglied der Kameradschaft Salzburg-Stadt
der Tapferkeitsmedaillenträger Österreichs
der Freiwilligen Schützen
des Verbandes der Südtiroler in Salzburg

am Montag, dem 31. Dezember 1979, versehen mit den Tröstungen der heiligen Kirche, im 81. Lebensjahr im Herrn entschlafen ist.

Wir verabschieden uns am Montag, dem 7. Jänner 1980 um 16 Uhr in der Aussegnungshalle auf dem Kommunalfriedhof in Salzburg.

Die heilige Seelenmesse feiern wir anschließend um 19 Uhr in der Stadtpfarrkirche von St. Martin.

In Liebe und Dankbarkeit:

KARL WINTER

Schwester IRMA   HEDDA und BERTA

mit ihren treuen Freunden und Bekannten

71

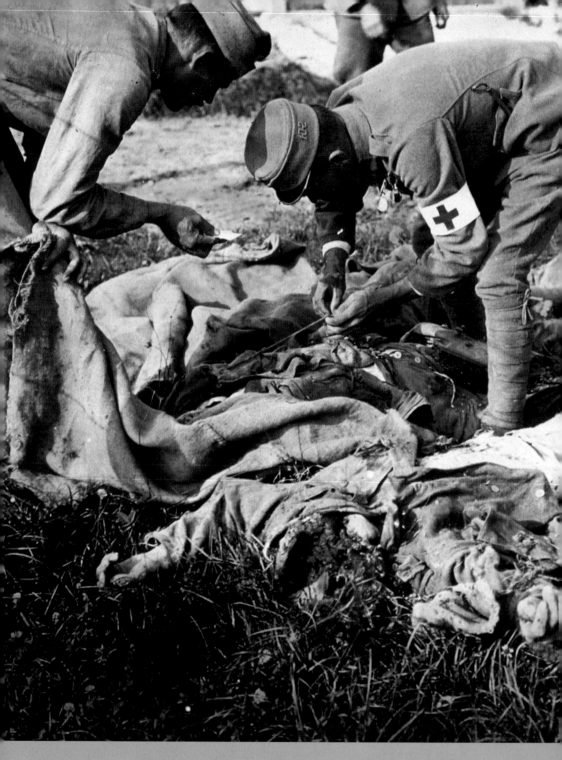

The colours of war

The Austrian imperial army photographer Richard Synek painstakingly added colour to 260 lantern slides. On behalf of the Austrian high command he frequented the bloody sites of the First World War including the Tyrolean front. The almost macabre sequence of especially sanguinary scenes makes the collection striking. Synek had few equals capable of portraying this war with all its grim realities.

73

Perfectly normal insanity

Lost in thought, the Czech-Austrian photographer Richard Synek gazes on the city of Trieste. Thereafter he became a war photographer charged with documenting the conflicts on the southern front. Syneck produced impressive pictures bringing home the true horrific reality of the war. All photographs: Stato Maggiore Esercito – Ufficio Storico Roma / Museo della Grande Guerra-Rovereto.

A train of covered wagons struggles through the quagmire towards the front. Supply routes especially caused enormous logistical problems for all frontline soldiers. After the war Richard Synek showed these photos which had originally been taken on glass plates to a large public to present his "war experiences from Italy". By chance the glass plates reached the historical archives of the Italian army staff and were subsequently made available to a wider public by the director of the War Museum of Rovereto, Dr. Camillio Zadra.

Emergency makeshift shelters were constantly erected. The idyllic scenes overlay the reality, for the conditions of hygiene often left much to be desired. The bottle of Italian wine also gives a misleading impression of comfort, for such a simple tent afforded little protection from rain and cold.

A village in Val Sugana after constant shelling. Bitter fighting took place above all in the area of Folgaria, Lavarone, the 'Seven Villages' and around the Pasubio massif resulting in the destruction of an immense number of villages. The Val Sugana connecting Trento with the Veneto plain at Vicenza provided the so-called Austro-Hungarian 'Punitive Campaign' with a means of breaking deep into Italian territory. Richard Synek painstakingly coloured all photographs by hand in order to imbue them with even greater force of expression.

Richard Synek entitled this romantic photograph "A Landscape in Tyrol". A cloud-veiled moon contributes to impart a surreal atmosphere the picture. Above all the presentation of general paralysis caused by the war, the uninhibited display of death in often idyllic surroundings engenders a unique sense of timelessness. The pictures became memorials as warnings to future generations. Synek came from a Jewish family in Bohemia. Many of his relations died in concentration camps during the Second World War.

Both the Austrians and Italians had built roads hurriedly to ensure supplies and rein-forcements. Countless columns of troops labour to carry supplies behind the Tyrolean lines up to the well-fortified front.

A lookout position has been excavated in the rock. This tastefully decorated and sturdily built hut was an exception. In most cases shelters were wooden constructions which could not even withstand the vagaries of the winter.

This snow-bound shelter beneath a rock comes closer to reflecting the reality. It was often impossible, especially in winter, to keep troops in these high regions supplied with the bare essentials - food, fuel and other materials.

A group of Kaiserjäger
have made themselves as
comfortable as possible
in this makeshift shelter.
They are waiting for
their next orders, most
probably guard duties,
reconnaissance tours or
organising supplies.
There were far fewer
combat actions during
the winter months,
though soldiers were kept
in a constant state of
alert, for surprise attacks
could never be discount-
ed.

The snow-mantled
Dolomite mountains in
winter. The principal
defences run along the
main ridge, behind which
huts and supply stores
are located out of dan-
ger. It is a position like
many others. However,
the Austro-Hungarians
enjoy the advantage of
having occupied the
highest summits and
strategically most impor-
tant positions. In addi-
tion the defenders were
fighting on their own
home territory which
they knew like the
proverbial backs of their
hands.

Static warfare involved eternal waiting and guard duties for the soldiers. A surprise enemy attack could result in the position being stormed at any moment. And if the enemy did not attack there were other opponents to contend with: hunger and thirst, cold and heat, homesickness and the many smaller, cruel banes which thrived in their millions in the filthy shelters and trenches in the form of lice and other pests which made soldiers' lives unbearable. There was nothing for it but to pluck them one by one from one's clothing.

Above: effort, courage and valour were rewarded with medals. However the lustre of these decorations could not mask the horrors of battle. Below: Austrian soldiers receive their rations. The containers were called 'Goulash cannons'. Like in other forces, in the Austrian Imperial Army the food prepared for common soldiers contrasted considerably with that served to the officers. These class differences were maintained until the war's end and were often a cause of odium and friction.

Above: dug-outs were built using limestone boulders, behind which the men barricaded themselves. The front in the mountains was soon reduced to enervating static warfare. Foxholes became uncomfortable soldiers' 'billets' for years on end. Below: a shell explodes on the front line. Sometimes in the high mountains only a few metres separated the enemies. Cases of the two sides fraternising were very frequent. Commanders were often changed as a countermeasure.

Above: the First World War was the first conflict in history in which the technology for killing became constantly perfected. For the first time machine guns were employed in large numbers. Below: hundreds of Italian soldiers are escorted into captivity. Italian morale reached an all time low following the their catastrophic defeat at Caporetto. Millions of mostly young Italians were used as cannon fodder on the battlefields, mowed down while attempting to break through the Austrian lines which were strategically better positioned.

Moving 'colour photographs' from the Austrian-Italian front in the First World War. These recently discovered documents were taken by the Czech photographer Richard Synek who coloured the glass plates by hand and showed them on lecture tours after the war. His announcements for his slide talks now sound macabre: "I extend a sin-

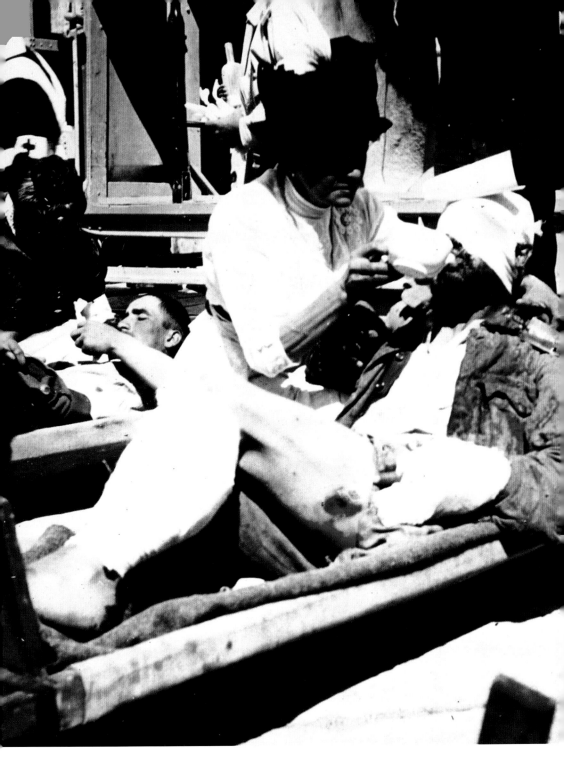

*cere welcome to all who have come today to hear about my war experiences in Italy
.... Witnesses bring along your wives, your children and grandchildren and show them
for the last time the places where you fought".*

After each battle, each attack, it was the turn of the medical orderlies. The wounded had to be rescued and taken to a field hospital. There they were given emergency treatment but often had to wait hours to be removed from the battlefield. Death often arrived sooner than the physician.

Large numbers of wounded lie on the ground after an attack, having only been admin-istered first aid. Often simple non-fatal injuries led to death due to the difficulty of providing emergency treatment to the wounded.

A civilian is hanged. Richard Synek belonged to the minority ethnic group of Czech Jews. An Austro-Hungarian law dictated that there should never be more than 8,600 Jewish families living in Bohemia. To this end only the eldest son of a Jewish family was allowed to marry while the others had to wait for a sib to die out or for a family to remain childless. This meant that many couples cohabited but their relationship was not recognised as a marriage.

A saboteur is hanged. Show trials were very common, used to intimidate the civil population. Both soldiers and the village populations were forced to witness the cruel executions. Above all the Austro-Hungarian monarchy with its multi-ethnic population and the suppressed interests of many nationalities was distrustful of the patriotic sentiments of individual language groups. Hangings and executions by firing squad were therefore the order of the day.

The hangman from Vienna was notorious and his services were often called upon. His cruelty and cynicism were particularly infamous, qualities which were given full rein when he was dealing with irredentists from Trentino. In addition to hanging and strangulation, death by firing squad was a frequent method of execution.

After the execution. A curate performs the last rites, members of the firing squad inspect their work while the onlookers begin to disperse. Desertion, sabotage and spying were all common among the non-German population in the Austro-Hungarian multi-ethnic state. Anybody who was caught was brought before a drumhead court-martial and executed within a few hours.

Graves are dug for the fallen. The dead await burial in long rows, though large numbers were left where they had fallen when it proved impossible to inter them with dignity.

Austrian soldiers have just captured an enemy position and have their photographs taken. Italian dead lie all around in the trenches. Below: Richard Synek titles this photograph "The comrade killed in action".

A last memorial to a fallen comrade. Sometimes it is a simple grave amid an idyllic landscape, in other cases hastily dug graves in a new cemetery. Many of these final resting places are consigned to oblivion and neglect.

We are making peace
The eighteen year-old Standschütze Karl Mayr and his diary of a soldier longing for peace

'The Rescuer'. An Italian Alipni solder, recognisable by his hat, has fallen down a rock face and an Austrian medical orderly administers first aid to him.

Günther Obwegs, Gottfried Leitgeb

Standschützen militia celebrating Mass on the Plätzwiese. Above all the Standschützen were deeply religious. They often said the rosary or celebrated Mass before and after a battle. Their profound faith was often mocked by officers and other units.

Arch. Fabio Ortolani - foto A. De Marinis

An Italian soldier lost in thought, without a rifle, equipped only with an alpenstock; he is looking from the Nuvolau towards the Tofana, Castelletto and Col Dei Bois.

Karl Wilhelm Mayr died in June 1962 in the neighbourhood of Vienna. He was a lawyer and died of a sudden massive heart attack. Throughout his lifetime he never made even the slightest mark in history, though since his death he has risen in prominence because of his unpublished diary. He wrote it for his fellow human beings but, unable to find a publisher who appreciated the worth of his thoughts, never managed to have it printed. His children safeguarded his typed manuscripts. Karl Wilhelm Mayr's life story can be quickly summarised: He was born the son of a forester at Gerlos in Tyrol on 6th January, 1897. His father died of cancer when he was a child. His mother subsequently married a 'Welsch-Österreicher', or 'Italian Austrian' from Rovereto in southern Trentino, then part of South Tyrol. From his step-father Karl Wilhelm learnt to speak Italian perfectly and the knowledge of both languages provided him with insight into the mores of both nations, an advantage which few of his compatriots shared. Every part of his diary expresses a longing for peace between the two warring parties even in the face of the most horrendous slaughter. Another aspect of Karl Wilhelm Mayr's story is important here: he volunteered to fight in the Standschützen – the Tyrolean civil defence militia - aged seventeen along with fifty other friends and schoolmates, all seduced by the offer of a 'Matura' school leaving certificate, the general qualification for university entrance. Only nine were to return alive. Karl Wilhelm Mayr lived through the entire war on the Dolomite front and became an impartial chronicler of events. He subsequently made his living as a respectable lawyer in the employ of the Austrian state railways, though with a little more self-confidence he could have have made a name for himself as an author. And so it has fallen to us to publish this diary. His most expressive sentences and thoughts have been extracted to enable something new to appear from the depths, providing an account which narrates aspects of this war far better than many others, permeated by the young Standschütze Karl Mayr's desperate longing for a little peace in that awful war.

A new epoch begins with terrible labour pains – World history is the world court – Evening has come – Anonymous suffering – Peace on earth to men of good will

The war began long before the actual war. When the sixteen year-old Karl Mayr travelled to his stepfather's home village, Lizzana on the southern out-skirts of Rovereto in summer 1913 the harbingers of the Great War followed him constantly. He was astonished to find that border defences were being built everywhere on the high plateau of Folgaria overlooking the Adige and Val Sugana valleys. All this in spite of the fact that neighbouring Italy was still a close ally of imperial Austria. "A massive fort has been built on Monte Cherle opposite San Sebastiano". The situation was similar on the Italian side. "A vir-tually identical one had appeared in the distance on the facing mountainsides of the Val Sugana farther south in Italian territory". The Mayr family were idylli-cally happy for the last time, and they spent their final holiday together in the home village of the children's stepfather, a man who, after their natural father had died of cancer, had treated the by then sixteen year-old Karl and his younger brother Artur with loving care as if they were his own.

The Great War did not come suddenly and as a shock. It had been seeming-ly longed for, governments did whatever they could to engender mutual suspi-cion and mistrust, nobody cared for alliances or treaties they had entered into. Everything pointed towards war even though there were no end of peace attes-tations to the point of ludicrousness. The previous state of monotonous coexis-tence would end, to allow splendid new empires to emerge from the rubble, or so many people thought. "This year in March the government decreed that all secondary school youths aged 16 and over can be given preliminary military training in the interest of national defence". Each nation began to set its propa-ganda machine in motion to put its people in the mood for the war, imminent though still a year away. Youths who were basically still children were trained to become soldiers and practise military discipline – a virtue to be strived for – driven until they collapsed.

The sixteen year-old youth Karl observed the activity from the protective cocoon of his family circle, while his insecure soul was torn between hope and despair. "National leaders knew that difficult times lay ahead the outcome of which would to be life or death, for the note of discord in the concert of European peoples was by then so deafening as to be impossible to ignore. Throughout the Austrian Empire an arms race had started and one had the dark feeling that the storm was about to break, it was only a question of where and when, for the situation had become far too explosive". People craved for a mil-itary campaign, the like of which had never been seen before, to bring about a better world order. And at last when the fatal shots of Sarajevo rang out: "The birth of a new epoch began with excruciating labour pains, a era with no stabilising element for the continued existence of the family". Accepted principles which had evolved over so much time with so much effort and sacrifice, a sense of honour, respect and other values were now about to be swept away in a storm of blood, while a propaganda machine whose wheels ground everything in its path was set in motion from on high with only one intention: to create bombastic illusions of one's own strength and denigrate the enemy, people who had became objects of scorn more through chance than well-deserved hate.

"World history is the world court. But this tribunal has handed down an irrevocable miscarriage of justice, condemning a whole generation of humanity to a punishment it has not merited". Many people felt like this but they were only small cogs in an enormous machine, with decisions being handed down from on high. For the events of 1914 were to make a whole generation to penitents. The seventeen year-old youth Karl Mayr observed his world from the small sleepy town of Hall in Tyrol as if he were at the umbilicus of the decisions. He sensitively observed even the smallest gesture both within himself and without, grasping desperately at every straw which could contain a redemptive element of peace. But he had to wait long, longer than anybody had anticipated. Everywhere people were in a state of wartime euphoria, the like of which had never been seen before and hardly anybody – not even Karl Mayr – sensed that they were headed towards disaster. People were too confident, being embedded in strong nations, feeling they were fighting in a just cause with God on their side. Very few became admonishers in the midst of this delirium, having realised that the fabric of old Europe had had its day and was already revealing deep and abysmal fissures.

"And so it happened at the time that, in the thick of events, we often mistook cause for effect and were no longer able to distinguish consistently between facts and potentiality. We were even misinformed about the actual causes of this immense conflict. We realised only much later that the revolver shots in Sarajevo were not the cause of the war but merely the starting pistol for a conflagration which had long been inevitable. It would have happened even without the events of Sarajevo, perhaps a few months later, but the fuse to the powder keg had already been lit and it had to explode".

Nobody guessed that young Karl Mayr would become a chronicler of such sensitive thoughts and feelings – like a shooting star hardly noticed by anyone – and whose destiny it was to burn out quickly leaving not a trace. In the wake of the events in Sarajevo, throughout Tyrol and elsewhere in Austria a period began in which patriotic demonstrations were organised, for the most part encouraged by the authorities. The blind crowds were to made even blinder, while the few dissenters and nonconformists were silenced or often even dismissed as lunatics. The old grey-haired district judge of Hall in Tyrol refused to be intimidated and held a moving and dignified valediction address. His words became drowned out in the general frenzy of war. "The evening is drawing in and darkness is falling on peace among the nations of Europe. We do not yet know what will happen but we must hold out until a new epoch dawns. A black night lies before us which will cost people much blood, sweat, distress, misery and wretchedness. I feel we are at a turning point in history".

These prophetic words made a lasting impression on the young Karl Mayr. He adopted them in the knowledge that the world would change. Confidence in the war still prevailed. People believed rumours and news items which were always far from the truth. Some said they had seen Italian troops coming to help the Austrians. A macabre fallacy.

The mood reached its climax at railway stations as young men, their country's lifeblood, mustered in their thousands to go to war. Men joined up certain to return quickly as heroes.

"They were all splendid country lads in their hechtgrau ('pike grey') uniforms and decked with flowers, they even had flowers stuck in the barrels of their rifles". Newspapers appeared as orgiastic special editions when there was good news. Sometimes several times a day. Towns and villages were decorated with flags whenever there was a report of a historic victory, for days on end when reports of triumphs came thick and fast. The extent of the tragedy unfolded when the first dead were brought home, and reports of recurrent horrors on the eastern front could no longer be hushed up. When mothers and fathers felt their sons had been stolen from them. In that moment the populace began to look behind the scenes and were horrified. But by then it was too late. Commanders and generals had already taken the helm, ordinary people became anonymous numbers, expendable cannon fodder. Young Karl Mayr had yet to mature, he observed and learnt. The exciting, optimistic reports began to run out: "They became more cover-ups of important setbacks and ingenious glossings-over of defeats rather than outright lies and misrepresentations of events". As time went on he became increasingly sceptical about the veracity of these reports. He became a subtle observer of events with an openness the like of which few others could match in a war such as this.

"The first official casualty lists were published in the autumn of 1914. With their hundreds upon hundreds of fallen soldiers' names, they finally brought home the dreadful seriousness of the war and indescribable grief struck many families which had lost their fathers or sons. The toll of lives during the first months of the war was especially heavy for Tyrol, whose elite regiments almost literally bled to death in the Galicia* battles". The drama of war

*Galicia was an Austrian province straddling what is now the Ukraine and Poland.

reached even the smallest villages and hamlets, it affected every farmstead. Although most people still believed in victory, even a quick victory with peace returning by Christmas, the fact that young men in their prime had to be continually replenished with those who had already escaped with their lives the first time made many families perplexed.

Karl Mayr soon realised that could no longer resist being swept along by the fatal flood tide of the war. He had no choice but to go with the flow, to row together with the others. Not even old enough to fight, he too became an instrument of war. Although he recognised that "diplomacy and warfare have nothing to do with morality but are in reality concepts and turns of fate which evolve and take place" beyond good and evil. Doubts and rebounding accusations nevertheless arise in his accounts like cruel mirrors of the truth. "The hostage of the war is to be found less in the physical hardships, but rather much more in the lifting of millenniums-old divine commandments. War has changed the Commandment 'Thou shalt not kill' into the commandment: 'Thou shalt kill'. The excuse that this killing in war is basically self-defence cannot be accepted. Only the attacked can act in the case of self-defence. But who is the aggressor and who the victim in war? Sometimes these roles alternate so rapidly that they can hardly serve as a criterion for ethical exoneration".

The full force of the war's impartial injustice was borne everywhere. He complained bitterly that "in Budapest there are still small baskets of snow-white bread rolls on restaurant tables, while in Tyrol from now on we have to survive on mouldy lumps of cornbread". There was no properly managed distribution centre, the longer the war lasted the more everybody tried to save what could be saved. The black market thrived, while the hording of food and other essential goods went on to an unimaginable extent. It was hopeless to expect justice in war, laws were always dictated by reality and the interests of the most powerful figures of the moment.

Prospects of an early peace were no longer a reality. "It is true that we celebrated the first Christmas of the war in our intimate family circle beneath the Christmas tree, though the homely atmosphere for this joyous festival was lacking. There was no 'peace on earth to men of good will', for on the eastern front the thunder of thousands of big guns rumbled on, the machine guns hammered away and thousands of young men were meeting a dreadful death".

White-bearded old men who hit with unbelievable accuracy – Wonders in the mountains – Their little flags flapped blithely in the morning wind – They were still gentlemen

Day by day news came increasingly thick and fast that Italy was preparing for war. But on the side of the enemy. It gradually dawned on everybody that there was nobody in position to defend the nation's southern frontier. For the homeland's defenders were rotting thousands of kilometres away in the east as attackers. "In Tyrol we told ourselves that our mountains formed a natural defensive bastion which could not easily be overrun, but nevertheless without men in place even the mountains could not defend themselves". The country resorted to a last ditch stand by a regiment of old men and youths, an army of defenders with a tradition deep-rooted in history: the Standschützen or civil defence militia. They may have resembled Don Quixote rather than an army, equipped with antiquated rifles but they were fighting for a higher ideal and purpose: to protect their homeland.

"The Tyroleans who had never endured bondage, had had their own Schützen – civil defence - companies in their individual villages since medieval times. This was made possible because the bearing of arms had never been forbidden in Tyrol, a special privilege which the Tyroleans clung to tenaciously and which they were also able to justify in an emergency. Anybody arriving in a Tyrolean village on a Sunday was almost certain to hear the crack of rifle fire emanating from the shooting range – even the smallest village had one - and knew that the Schützen were practising. These civil defence companies were organised on military lines under the command of officers chosen by the members. They were for the most part men capable of bearing arms, from youths to white-haired old men who still hit their targets with amazing accuracy on the shooting range. These 'Schützen' formations were called up in times of danger when the homeland was threatened by interlopers." Above all the knowledge that the homeland's borders were being threatened was reason enough to mobilise the last reserves. Young Karl Mayr became enthusiastic about what he considered was a just cause.

"We wanted to leave the classroom behind and prove that we too were young men who could help the fatherland." Both young and old voluntarily swelled the ranks in the service of their home country which was under attack. From then on the task was not to fight an unknown country – like on the eastern front – but to protect one's own home mountains and nothing more. This is where the legendary 'Wonder in the Mountains' was born. There was no holding back once Karl Mayer and other students heard that in the case of front line action they would be absolved of the need to complete the school year. He applied to the commander of the Standschützen of Hall, the painter Hans Fuchs – a prime example of non-professional, elected officers leading the territorial defence forces, a phenomenon which characterised the subsequent fighting: "I explained my request to this man modestly and hesitantly, mentioning that I was a student at the Hall grammar school. He looked at me kindly with his milk-blue eyes and said:

"But of course I'll gladly accept you into my unit, but tell me, how old are you?" Karl Mayer had to tell the truth, that he was not yet eighteen. He was instructed to return with the signature and consent of his parents. His mother signed with a heavy heart. His Italian-speaking stepfather was serving on a distant front and gave his consent by telephone. Adolescent Karl Mayr's life changed on that day. During the following days the recruits were accoutred, hurriedly taught the basics of shooting. The motley collection of troops comprising students, old farm workers and craftsmen were trained in the most fundamental military principles. An army of unlikely soldiers gradually formed an effective unit. Their captain, called Schiessl, weighed at least 100 kilos, was an innkeeper, "and if he sleeked his martial moustache – we thought – the Italians would certainly shake in their boots". They were advised to buy tonics from the chemist's to combat potential states of anxiety, then they were off marching southwards to an unknown destination in the direction of the Italian border. "On the march our company was an impressive column of almost 300 men. Our captain Schiessl rode in front on his heavy horse and set the pace. He let us rest frequently out of consideration for the numerous older men – after all there were many aged between 50 and 60 – and for the heavy equipment we had to carry."

A final ostensibly daunting troop formed up courageously to accomplish the task they had been assigned. They were handed live ammunition, then had their photograph taken as a peaceful group. Nobody knew at the time whether this would be the last picture for their loved ones. They were first of all informed that they would be deployed at Sexten in the Pustertal valley. Their mission on the front line was to stop the invading Italians. For the glory of their fatherland and homeland of Tyrol. "We worked hard on reinforcing the fortifications during the following weeks. To us greenhorns they seemed safe and strong and we were in no doubt that we could defend them effectively. In reality though, in the face of a formidable attack with accompanying artillery fire, even with supreme feats of gallantry we would never have been able to hold a position for even two hours, for we had no artillery, nor even machineguns." Each helped as best he could to stop the invading enemy. Old men and youths alike. Their idol was Andreas Hofer, the Tyrolean hero who had led their forefathers against the Bavarian and French occupying forces in 1809.

Fortunately the Italians hesitated. Large numbers of troops were unsure who they were supposed to be fighting. Life could have been less burdensome. "Each day we expected the Italians to attack but days and weeks passed without anything in particular happening on our narrow front section." Nothing much happened throughout the month of June, giving the Standschützen troops time to dig trenches and engage in basic military training. Initially they needed to be fully alert to avoid shooting each other. They were far too inexperienced to be able to distinguish friend from foe at night. The chaplain, a Czech priest, assured them in glowing words that they would go straight to heaven while at the same time passionately damning the enemy to hell. Karl was not completely convinced by this attitude.

The Sexten mountains were still unknown terrain for them and the one or other soldier still wandered inadvertently into enemy territory only to fight his way back in the direction of his own positions. Otherwise not much happened. Suddenly at the beginning of July the situation became serious, the real war began. Karl Mayr was astonished. One day around one hundred riders in brightly-coloured uniforms and in regimented formation trotted up to the Kreuzberg pass. It seemed as if they intended to take Vienna in a daring assault. "They were Italian lancers, so-called 'lanzieri' and their flags fluttered gaily in the morning wind. We wanted to open fire but our acting sergeant wouldn't let us. He wanted to wait and see what would follow and ordered us to form a firing line and to cover ourselves well. Having reached the tollhouses the enemy cavalry troop stopped, the riders dismounted and tethered their horses to the trees. The soldiers took their entrenching tools and began to dig trenches beside the road. We couldn't believe our eyes at such a lack of experience in mountain warfare, for as far as we could see they didn't even post lookouts. At last our acting sergeant gave us the orders to open fire. We gave them all our guns were capable of in a sudden barrage of well-aimed rifle fire at the horses and unsuspecting working cavalry men. The confusion we caused was immense. Initially they all ran around chaotically and when the first dead and wounded lay in the road they fled for cover behind the customs houses from where they opened fire blindly and haphazardly, though completely in the wrong direction without troubling us in the slightest. When we had no further targets we retreated and disengaged from the enemy unchallenged. At least a dozen lay dead or wounded at the customs houses as well as a number of horses."

For Karl Mayr the massive slaughter and, in effect, the real war began like a comic play. In the evening the youths were praised for their courage and quickly fell exhausted onto their hard beds. However the respite was brief, they were soon ordered to sally forth. Italian Alpinis had established a position up on the Seikofl summit. A few days later respectable gentlemen joined them to perform their duty in what they themselves named the 'Academic Legion'. They expected to be addressed with their professional and academic titles and most of these sages taught at Innsbruck University or worked as physicians, lawyers or scientists. In the meantime, as a precaution they ordered their students to dig themselves into the loamy soils on the Alpine pastures as protection against enemy fire. After several hours they stood knee-deep in the holes they had dug themselves, completely covered in dirt.

Still, they proved themselves to be novices in the art of warfare. "When I crawled back into my foxhole after midnight a young lance corporal belonging to our 4th platoon came to me and I took a liking to him immediately. He gave me two hand grenades which proved to be such primitive improvisations, each consisting of barbed wire wound around a metal capsule fixed to a piece of board, that I asked what I was supposed to do with them. He answered:

'Yes my old fruit, I haven't a clue either. Just chuck one on top of them if they come here!'".

Soldiers on both sides now suddenly stood face to face, the attackers and defenders and awaited events. On the other hand, pitched battles were already being fought in the area of the Drei Zinnen. The soldiers heard shots and explosions. The revered mountain guide Sepp Innerkofler fell during those days. Karl Mayr recounted respectfully how the Italians had even made him a gravestone. "Both sides still consisted of gentlemen in this mountain war. It should be stressed that the Alpinis on the Italian side who were put into action in the high mountains were valiant, splendid troops who were magnificently up to the task assigned them. These Alpinis were no easy adversaries. They were tough soldiers used to the mountains, recruited exclusively from the Italian Alps. They fought ferociously metre by metre, rock face by rock face."

Nevertheless the brave volunteer defence troop would have been quickly overrun in spite of all their courage had they not been rescued by the German Alpine Corps. The foreign troops, mainly from the Bavarian Alps, were still not officially at war with Italy, but subsequently proved most adept at working together with these rural soldiers who they slowly transformed into an effective fighting force with profound intuition. For the wave of attacks increased both in intensity and strength after July 1915. The Italians had amassed thousands of soldiers along the front line and were concentrating all their efforts on penetrating into the Pustertal valley via the Kreuzberg pass and the Sexten valley.

Like a primeval animal – I began to weep like a child – Some stared at the sky with bloodshot eyes – Heroes only exist in fiction

"Violent, blinding thunderbolts struck in the immediate vicinity with primeval clashes, I had to unfix my bayonet because it began to crackle with electricity. St. Elmo's fire illuminated the barbed wire defences and when the watch commander came to me briefly his beard glowed and crackled so uncannily that he seemed like a primeval animal creeping towards me. Then the heavens opened with a lashing deluge and I was wet to the skin within minutes. However, as if that was not enough, in the midst of this weather chaos the sound of furious infantry fire suddenly pealed from the Sarre ridge guard. After almost five minutes it stopped just as abruptly as it had started. For God's sake, something must have happened out there! Our guard troops had probably been attacked and a good half of them were our Standschützen. But given the prevailing conditions we were unable to come to their aid and had no choice but to wait and see.

"It was no wonder that in this situation, around midnight, suddenly I almost suffered a physical and mental breakdown. I began to cry like a child, trembled in all my limbs and went back to the watch officer who was situated 20 paces behind me. I told him he could do with me what he wanted, but I couldn't go on. He was an old Standschützen platoon commander whose name I can no longer remember, but was a sprightly, lusty Tyrolean mountain farmer who with an affecting humanity said: 'But son, what's the point of bursting out in tears. Lay down for a while in my foxhole, take a rest and when you've composed yourself again go and fix the defences. You needn't leave the position anymore tonight. I'll go out'."

From then on the war bared its brutish teeth which would soon sink into the sanguine young troops. The powers of nature seemed to have conspired against them just as it had against the Italian troops who were becoming increasingly better organised. The first dead in their platoons shocked both sides equally. "It was the Standschütze called Klingenschmid, a farmer from the Vomperberg mountain. Ill-fatedly a spoon in his lunch bag was torn into his abdomen by a bullet." A pair of 20 year-old identical twins died likewise in a hail of bullets. Artur Wallpach, a poet in the above mentioned academic group, set them a literary monument in his verses.

Death took unpredictable and diverse forms. Their dry tongues stuck to their palates, day after day they crawled around the swampy ground on the Kreuzberg pass without food while they burrowed in the mud like moles. After an attack some trenches looked like a crater field. Even the older and hardened Standschützen suffered and showed their feelings. "They kept quiet and apparently pulled themselves together and mustered all their strength to get over the unavoidable psychological effects of shock, though some stared up to the sky with bloodshot eyes hoping that the terrible roar of the heavy bombardment would stop." Their positions were initially shelled by the Italians, seemingly in preparation for an assault. Hundreds upon hundreds of shells rained down on them in an inferno and landed just anywhere. The spot where Karl Mayr had been sitting and where he had spread out his sheep's wool blanket was reduced a few seconds later to a few rags and a crater. By chance he had left the position for a moment. This war began to drain the young Standschützen. Even the village of Toblach was bombarded. They had to sleep mostly on the damp ground and the night became full of agonising unforeseeable events. "For a while I lay in a somewhat forward foxhole and peered out into the darkness. Our position commander had warned us for God's sake not to fall asleep, for ten days earlier a Kaiserjäger had nodded off for a moment, exhausted in the same trench and was stabbed stealthily by an enemy scouting patrol."

Only Bavarian companies who had trained on the battlefields of Flanders raised the army's moral and initiated these troops of farmers into new war tactics. The latter were more than willing pupils. Nevertheless each day a soldier survived he thought of as his lucky day. "I had hardly been half a minute in my position when a heavy shell howled down and hit the Schützen position directly where I had been standing less than a minute earlier. Shivers ran down my spine and I sent a sincere honest prayer of thanks up to Heaven."

In these first months of the war Karl Mayr already lost all illusions of heroism and supermen. He became a rational human being who clung to anything which could somehow enable him to get through the day. "The kind of heroes who were left untouched by all such terrifying events and experiences exist only in fiction, not in reality and I have heard men subjected to constant bombardment from whose mouths otherwise only blasphemies issued forth praying in fear of death."

He became a perspicacious observer and turned his attention equally to nature. He found a small lake in the Hollbruck Valley, such rich blue in colour that it appeared to him almost unreal. It seemed as though "the lake bottom was formed of bright malachite". Keen spiritual emotions suddenly began to burgeon within him like magical powers. The amiable, kind-hearted mountain priest from Hollbruck in East Tyrol made an indelible impression on him because in an act of selflessness he gave his shoes to a Standschütze whose own were full of holes, then walked down the stony pathway to the valley barefoot. Beforehand the priest had uplifted all present with his ardent words of encouragement. Or the peace-loving cow which grazed continuously between the two enemy lines, or the grating call of the ptarmigans which were among the few wild creatures which held out up there on the front line after all others had been frightened away by shellfire and bullets.

In these days the young Standschützen soldiers matured into men who only rarely showed their inner feelings. They remained strong even when more and more older Standschützen descended to the valley weakened and marked by the strain. They wanted to be real men even though they were hardly eighteen years old. They began to drink alcohol and to smoke to show they were true men. "We had definitely lost weight but had become tougher and wirier, and our senses were more acute because of the constant danger and our natural way of life. During the night we could hear the slightest sound a good kilometre away and our eyes too noticed the smallest movement or change."

We thought the end of the world had come – A soldier was just a tiny cog in the machine – Here and there an arm protruded from the soil – Release from agony with a well-aimed coup de grâce

The life of the trusty Standschütze Karl Mayr was to change fundamentally on 14th August 1915*. For on this day the war assailed him and hundreds of others with a violence and a "hurricane of hell which could hardly have been more intense". Soon there was hardly a square metre of ground on the Roteck mountain overlooking the Kreuzberg pass which had not been churned up by artillery fire. The Italian troops had received orders from the general staff to concentrate their forces, break through the Austrian lines and penetrate into the open Pustertal valley via the Sextental. They were convinced that they would only meet with weak resistance here and that the assault was certain to succeed. Initially the wretched defending troops were pinned down in the caverns excavated in the sandstone which were fortunately almost completed. Shells rained down on them and left enormous craters. The defensive positions on the China saddle were to be weakened by a softening-up barrage in preparation for an attack.

The Italian troops had massed all their resources. They pounded the positions with light and heavy artillery incessantly and apparently haphazardly. On the defensive side only a worn-out Belgian artillery gun performed its duty, but which proved more of a danger to the solders' own position than to that of the enemy. Finally after several days of intensive artillery bombardment the Italians were convinced that taking the mountain would be nothing more than a "military walkover, for nobody could be left alive up there on the Roteck", as the Italian prisoners, who had earlier served under the General Cantore, told the valiant Standschützen later. General Antonio Cantore, the initial commander of this front sector and notorious for his harshness and arrogance, was intent on laying the successful breakthrough to Vienna at the feet of his king as a gift. Cantore succeeded neither in this nor in escaping with his life. While on a reconnaissance tour of the front line a few weeks after the declaration of war a Tyrolean Standschütze shot him straight between the eyes, apparently much to the joy of many of Cantore's own troops. The order to attack was given. The soldiers were to advance in hundreds of columns for the glory of their fatherland. However, events produced a different outcome.

"The Italians made a catastrophic, fatal mistake at the very outset of their infantry attack. While at a distance they advanced in impressive broad lines, probably the way they had been taught on exercises, the closer they came to our positions the more they crowded together, providing us with mass targets of a

The actual date of the attack was 4th August, 1915

kind which our machine gunners could only dream of. It was probably a basic instinct in men to seek protection in crowds when the danger of death looms. Still it would be wrong to suppose that the Italian infantrymen were low in morale. They were simply inexperienced in high mountain warfare, a weakness for which they paid dearly. Even the Italian officers who led their men into battle with admirable courage and drawn sabres made the dreadful mistake of wearing their officer caps trimmed with gold braiding, recognisable from a distance by our snipers as priority targets. For this reason the Italians lost disproportionate numbers of officers during those days of fighting while in the forward front lines almost as many of them were shot as were the daring sappers who tried with varying success to blow up our barbed wire entanglements using Bangalore torpedoes."

What followed was a drama and slaughter in which Italy's finest young men were driven blindly to their deaths. "Hundreds upon hundreds of Italian soldiers were sent literally as cannon fodder to assault our positions, only to bleed to death on the steep Alpine meadows." The 'Eviva' cries of the Italian solders died away harrowingly in blood, the first major battle on this extended front ended in a bloodbath. For what the Standschützen were unable to manage with their primitive rifles was tackled by the eminently capable Alpenkorps machine-gunner. "This machinegun mowed down awesomely the Italian assault troops who increasingly massed together and we had no choice but to pick off individual soldiers." And the few who still managed to penetrate through to the forward positions on the Roteck were bayoneted. When the trenches began to fill they rolled "those who were hit down the mountainside".

When the Standschützen finally thought they had once more saved their skins for the day a horrendous artillery bombardment started all over again with such intensity "that we thought the end of the world had come. It was the most terrifying drumfire that I had to endure throughout the entire war." The guns flashed all around and from everywhere the shells rained down, showering the youths with stones and earth. They cowered, huddling close together in the trenches until in desperation Corporal Nitzlnader suddenly pulled a rosary from his trouser pocket.

"And he began to lead the prayers. Everyone of us devoutly joined in and it was wonderful how praying calmed us in the face of death. The horrific barrage lasted for over an hour." Each minute they survived seemed like a miracle to them. The mortar bombs struck all around them until the bombardment suddenly stopped at nine o'clock in the morning. Then they knew what would follow. "Again wave after wave of Italian assailants ran towards our trenches accompanied by the hoarse cry of 'Eviva' and 'Avanti Savoia'." Once again the Italians were driven to their deaths like lemmings. Again the machinegun on the China saddle rattled and fired until it suddenly went quiet. The valiant machine-gunner had been hit in the head. However for the moment the Italian troops were also shattered. The young Standschützen could not believe it.

"This went so well because the Italians stood out like silhouettes against the sky and we were able to keep tab on the effect of our shots, for the soldiers which had been hit rolled down the mountainside. In this way my friend Jud M. hit eight enemy in a short time, and I could claim five that I had definitely hit." But there was no respite as the Italian artillery once again began firing, though this time against their own troops, to whip the retreating soldiers back into action. Their situation was hopeless. Death bared its teeth before them, while from behind they were met with their own side's bullets.

"Less than 20 metres from our trench and Italian officer jumped out of a crater and obviously beside himself with rage, threw his sabre down the mountainside in the direction of the Italian positions, then collapsed riddled with bullets fired by our marksmen. After this demonstration of cruel inhumanity by the Italian artillery more and more Italians surrendered and entered our positions with their hands up."

It was only then that the Standschützen realised that they had almost run out of ammunition. They were suffering from thirst while the blazing August sun beat down on them. One of them volunteered to set out on the extremely hazardous errand to the rear positions. They wished him well, were sure that he had not survived when, to their surprise he returned heavily laden. Just in time. "The third Italian attack which started shortly after mid day no longer had the strength required to break through to our trenches. It was of short duration and when it broke down under our fire the completely exhausted enemy soldiers surrendered in droves."

And so the slopes on the Kreuzberg pass were soaked in blood, the courageous attack ended as a massacre. Dead and wounded lay everywhere. "By early afternoon the enemy artillery fire had ceased completely and we were able to emerge from our positions unhindered. The area in front was literally littered with fallen Italians and we were able to rescue some badly wounded after giving them first aid as best we could. An Italian captain who lay completely apathetic in a crater with both legs pierced in several places could not thank me enough and was visibly moved to be spoken to by me in his own language."

Four hundred Italians who had set out full of hope and certain of victory lay among the rocks. Dead. Plus many hundreds of wounded. The scent of death hung everywhere among the abandoned rifles and weapons. "When the sun had risen behind the grotesque peak of the Col Quaterna and bathed the summits and meadows with its light the entire front was quiet. The Italian positions lay there as if dead and not a shot rang out. We staggered to Hochgränten, took a few slurps of hot coffee and fell worn out onto our beds."

Karl Mayr was at the end of his tether. He wanted peace, his conscience and the search for the meaning of life tormented him. He wanted to find a different life. A better, more honourable, and above all, a peaceful existence. And he accused those who handed down the orders from on high, ensconced in luxurious rooms remote from the front and moved thousands of men backwards and forwards on drawing boards.

"In this First World War a soldier was still just a tiny cog in the enormous machine of a vast army. He hardly ever had a chance to act autonomously, take crucial decisions and behind the battle line he had no opportunity to form a coherent overview of events." He fervently tried to justify his own actions and that of the others. "All thought and speculative reflection were completely dismissed and one acted purely with one's senses in a frenzy." It was rare to hear such words in this war, written God knows not by a highly gifted poet or philosopher, but by an eighteen year-old volunteer.

"When Corporal Nitzlnader wrested the badly wounded comrade from the enemy in had-to-hand fighting on the Sarre ridge and hit out like a wild madman, or when an Italian officer led his men in an attack, undaunted with drawn sabre they were at heart not heroes however much they may seem to be. They were acting entirely instinctively as determined by their character and humanity. There is no hiding or dissembling in the face of extreme mortal danger, when men reveal their true selves. This reality is often completely different from the appearances of the conventional person." What binds them independent of nation, age or profession is their will to survive. As long as luck stays on their side.

"If a single shared experience can create intimacy, then how much more would the common feeling of staring death in the face create a close, profound bond between men who otherwise in normal life would hardly have noticed each other?" The events and feelings described here are not from a novel, but from an individual's genuine experiences. Not in the least embellished, but written down in impotent words as an appeal to future generations. Karl Mayer already anticipated the next calamity, the next war. For the present conflagration – he felt – was only the beginning of an even more dreadful conflict.

"If there is a war in the next century – and please God there won't be – it will be a pitiless war of mass destruction devoid of all human and spiritual feeling in which technical progress will decide the outcome. All individual initiative, bravery and heroism will be dispensed with. Perhaps such a war will be conducted on a chessboard, from which cosmic powers of destruction will be directed."

The more the honest Standschütze pondered, the deeper he penetrated into the depths of the human soul, where there the room for feelings and spiritual impulses became less and less. And he realised "that we front soldiers were not a conglomerate of friends, but rather a collection of comrades who had been forged into a unified whole in the utmost adversity, who had helped each other to the point of self sacrifice. This was the only way to endure such a destiny for weeks, months, even years".

For days the dead and even badly wounded lay around on the Sarre ridge. Italian politicians came and seemed more concerned about how to retrieve the dead soldiers' weapons rather than how to recover their bodies and bury them behind the lines with honour and dignity. They began to haggle and negotiate at length. When an agreement was reached and a six-hour ceasefire began the politicians gave the order to the medical orderlies to bury the dead any old how in the larger craters and fill them in as best they could without even planting wooden crosses. "Here and there an arm or foot projected from the earth." They were memorials to anonymity. The parliamentarians hurried away after they had failed to retrieve the rifles and artillery guns in spite of tough bargaining. The throngs of soldiers who were moved around like on a chessboard had done their duty and a new game could start. The commanders down in the valley were not interested in hearing about the expiring lives high up in the mountains. They were already concentrating on the next battles.

On new strategies and tactics. "Although calm prevailed that night on the Sarre ridge we had no peace. The reason being that several badly wounded Italians called out for help all night long from no-man's-land to the east of the Sarre but especially from the steep rocky slopes in front of the Demut mountain. Their cries of 'aiuto' resounded eerily through the night." Karl Mayr spoke Italian perfectly. He felt it his duty to rescue one of the wretched soldiers. Risking his life he crawled towards the Italian positions until he came within earshot. He made the enemy an offer. No one would shoot, they could rescue their wounded unharried. There would be a ceasefire lasting just a few minutes. However the other side only responded with the rattle of machine-gun fire. And so the wounded soldier lay dying, lonely in no-man's-land. He could still be heard two nights later, though his whimpering had become weaker.

He lay on a ledge clearly visible from all around. They tried but failed to rescue him. Then they considered compassionately "whether we should put him out of his misery with a well-aimed coup de grace. There were snipers among us for whom it would have been child's play but none of them could bring themselves to do it. And so this Italian soldier, who also had a mother and perhaps wife and children who worried about him had to die in agony and without help. It was then that the dreadful tragedy and cruelty of war struck me for the first time."

The hopes of all those who believed that this war would herald in a better epoch were dashed in death.

People who wore skirts – A shapeless mass of flesh and bones – He invited me to visit him when the war was over – A pile of louse-ridden, emaciated figures

Karl Mayr was exhausted, suffering from fever and bronchitis and he was developing severe pneumonia. He was advised to go down to the field hospital at Kartitsch. He struggled to get to Hollbruck by early evening. The kind-hearted mountain priest took him in affectionately and even offered him his own bed. However Mayr felt too unkempt and louse-ridden. Nevertheless he slept in a barn feeling like a prince in the hay. Then he walked on unsteadily to Sillian, for the field hospital was hopelessly overcrowded. For the first time in his life he was astonished to realise that the world had two different faces. "I stared almost in bewilderment at the humans wearing skirts. Women. It was such a long time since I had last seen members of the gentle sex, even though those country lasses working in the cornfields hardly merited the adjective 'gentle'."

He was deloused, after which he was allocated one of the beds with snow-white linen. "That was more magnificent and wonderful than paradise. I, who had slept on the ground for weeks and months louse-ridden and filthy by wind and weather, always expecting to have to jump up from my sleep and reach for my rifle was now supposed to lay in this white bed and nobody was allowed to disturb me."

However as a dutiful soldier the Standschütze Karl Mayr soon felt guilty living this inactive life and returned to the front and his comrades. To his unit which had started out with fifty men and now only counted sixteen. And each day another was missing. The young Standschütze took up smoking. Pipe, cigars - anything which glowed and ostensibly kept fear at bay. A typhoid epidemic even broke out on the Roteck. Then hostilities resumed again. The Italians were planning an attack which the dauntless Tyrolean soldiers feared would be even more horrendous than what had gone before. Many of his fellow combatants could no longer withstand the strain. "Cases of insanity increased and the makeshift cemetery on the Nemesalpe mountain grew."

Then came the 9th September, 1915*. "We, the last remaining members of the 3rd platoon of the Hall Standschützen were fast asleep." They were woken. Lietenant Erlacher, worse for wear for drink, ordered them to occupy the China saddle. They lit their pipes to steady their frayed nerves. It was a case of life or death. They wandered backwards and forwards on the front line under enemy fire and considered themselves lucky not to have been hit. A grazing shot knocked Karl Mayr's rifle to his knee with such force that he fell. He recovered and fled panting to the trenches on the Hochgränten. "And it was so cold that we wrapped our feet in rags to stop them freezing." The old gun had no recoil

*The actual date of the attack was 6th September, 1915

system and reared with each shot, causing the gunners to be thrown through the air head-over-heels with every shot. Confusion raged. An artillery sergeant stumbled towards them. " 'Crucifix Laudon! I've been hit!' In the hut he ripped his blood-soaked tunic and shirt open. He had been shot in a lung." Calm had to be restored in their own completely surprised division, for they knew that something horrific was about to start all over again. "What occurred over the next half hour was one of the most dramatic scenes that I saw and experienced in the entire Italian campaign." The Italians had occupied several trenches. Members of the Bavarian infantry regiment threw hand grenades into the trenches and surprised the enemy. Around two hundred Italians surrendered immediately. "Just a few seconds later an Italian officer jumped out of the machine-gun nest at the northern end of the China saddle and shot the Bavarian lieutenant with his pistol at point blank range. He rolled down the mountainside dead. The Bavarians were so furious at this that they forced their way in to the machine-gun position where, in shocking hand-to-hand fighting they stabbed to death all the Italian occupants with their knives. They beat the Italian officer with their rifle buts into a shapeless mass of flesh and bones. At first we were unable to understand this inhuman fit of rage and only heard their explanation about an hour later. It transpired that the lieutenant who was so treacherously shot after the Italians had surrendered was enormously popular among his team. His loss affected his soldiers personally to the point where they lost control of themselves and behaved like animals. Even the warrant officer who commanded the already mentioned mountain artillery unit was so angered by this occurrence that he had two mortar bombs fired into the group of Italians who had surrendered."

Karl Mayr was broken-hearted, at his wits' end. Once again several of his friends with whom he had gone to war full of ideals had died. His schoolmate Rudolf Reiter was hit in the spine, another school companion, Karl Schumacher lay on the ground with a bad penetration wound in the neck and a shattered upper arm, Corporal Nitzlnader lay dying, two others had fallen. Eighteen-year-old Rudolf Reiter survived long enough to reach the field hospital. They eased his dreadful agony with morphine, then his life too drew to a close.

"In the meantime an awful tragedy befell the enemy between the Roteck summit, the China saddle and the Sarre ridge. The Italians had forced almost three battalions of their 92nd infantry regiment into this space, corresponding to some 3,000 men, who became subjected to deadly machine-gun fire from three sides. Within minutes hundreds of dead and badly wounded bestrew the slopes of the Nemesalpe heights before hundreds finally surrendered and came towards our positions with their hands up." Less than three hundred men managed to return safely to their lines. Many surrendered demoralised.

"And still I and my schoolmates who had survived were not in the least happy about this victory, for the losses suffered by our platoon which had already become drastically reduced in number affected us greatly. Only ten of us remained and we felt like lost sheep. Ugh! This was no longer an optimistic war. We had seen the atrocious reality in the eyes of these hostages. On 9th September 1915* we finally saw the war for what it was, a fate we could not avoid, a grim duty which, for the time being, we could not escape. Still we believed we were fighting a just war – after all we were the ones who had been attacked and had to defend ourselves – but we felt it to be a harsh fate. No, it was not sweet to die for the fatherland. To describe eightteen-year-old youths in the prime of life bleeding to death in agony on the steep rocky slopes of this mountain as 'sweet' would have been a terrible blasphemy."

Some 2,000 dead and badly wounded lay round about in a tiny area on the Roteck, plus five hundred prisoners, twice as many men as all the Austrian troops there. They were pitiful pictures. "A Standschütze medical orderly was administering first aid to wounded Italians in the hollow beneath the Hochgränt saddle, where I noticed a tall Italian soldier who had been shot through the stomach. But strangely he was not lying on the ground but standing and contemplated his wound from above, almost apathetically with the orderly kneeing beneath him painting it with iodine before applying sticking plaster." A bullet had passed straight through his abdomen, exiting close to his spine. Karl Mayr wondered at many of these individual fortunes.

"A badly-wounded Italian captain with a jet-black pointed beard was brought to us on a stretcher. His body was wrapped in a blanket and he suppressed his obviously intense suffering courageously. With the most moving words he nevertheless took the chance to thank our soldiers and especially one of our officers for the humane way they had treated him. As a sign of his gratitude he wanted to give the orderlies two valuable rings which he was wearing on his pale, aristocratic fingers but they refused to accept them."

The dead were left where they had fallen, this time no politicians came to bargain. In the meantime killing had become a habit. Each side left it up to the sense of honour and morale of the other side to decide how and where to bury the fallen. Wounded were found even two days after a battle: "I approached him and noticed that the man really was still breathing. He had only been hit in the head and lay there unconscious. He was a tall soldier with a swollen but rather friendly face. Slowly we managed to bring him to, not least because I addressed him in his own language. He cried incessantly 'sete, sete' (thirst, thirst). But where were we supposed to find water? Then I noticed a small patch of old snow. We took some and melted it in one of the shell cases which were lying around and poured it into the poor wounded soldier's mouth. He actually came round, we bandaged his head wound and he could not thank us enough. He told

*The actual date of the attack was 6th September, 1915

us that he was the son of a rich landowner in the area of Vicenza, gave us his name and invited us, especially me, to visit him and his father after the war so he could show his gratitude. We then organised his removal and had the feeling we had done a good deed."

Still things happened which remained inexplicable and mysterious. "In these days I experienced another odd occurrence on the desolate battlefield of the Nemes-Alpe heights which to me is still an enigma. A dead Italian lay on the ground with his rifle beside him. But the lock on the rifle was sewn up with waxed cloth. This means that the soldier had knowingly gone into battle for some reason with an unusable weapon. But why?"

The few remaining troops who had started out so optimistic and full of hope were now to take their leave, of the Roteck and the Hochgränten saddle. For the first time they were allowed to go home. They were mature, had become men, toughened. But still with feelings.

"The deaths of some beloved comrades had moved us profoundly, but otherwise the bloody events of the 9th September* had dulled our feelings towards death – I would almost say it dissipated us spiritually. The sight of death, often accompanied by terrible wounds and the apathetic burying of human beings who still counted as being created in the image of God no longer touched us in the slightest. We had grown used to it, we came to regard it a matter of routine which no longer affected us. Life? What was life worth after all? A small case of steel with a piece of lead could extinguish this life. No rooster crowed, no tear was shed for it. It was nothing more than an annoying chore to have to dispose of the dead just any old how and it became even more of a nuisance when dozens of dead lay all around and the humus layer on the rocky ground was often only a few centimetres deep."

Karl Mayr found two books among the belongings of a fallen Italian officer and kept them. One contained various speeches by the Italian poet Gabriele D'Annunzio, the other verses by Giovanni Pappini printed on splendid deckle-edged paper. "I took great pains to work through these two books and began to imagine a new, different world full of breathtaking beauty. Gabriele D'Annunzio's speeches, especially the one held at Quarto, Genoa, was a masterpiece of poetic rhetoric and I could easily imagine how, in a young and healthy nation which had not yet achieved political maturity, such fanfare and oratory could elicit storms of enthusiastic applause. These rousing words must have released such energy as to seize an entire nation with elemental force and prompt them into action." Karl Mayr began to translate some of Giovanni Pappini's verses into German but quickly gave up. The "enchanting beauty of this language" was untranslatable. From Sexten they looked back once again into the past.

*The actual date of the attack was 6th September, 1915

"Once again we looked wistfully down to the China saddle which was soaked with the blood of our most beloved comrades…" Then it was time to take their leave. From a chapter which would mark them for life.

"Then the nine of us walked wide apart across the Hornischeck back into the rear. It was a pathetic platoon, this collection of emaciated, unkempt figures whose uniforms hung from their bodies like rags and whose worn-out shoes had holes showing their naked toes. What had happened to this proud column of school students which once comprised over 50 persons? A wretched handful of louse-ridden, wasted figures who crossed the mountain ridge gasping like worn-out hikers."

It is not sweet to die for the fatherland – On the cracked plinth of youthful ideals – Where was God?

They all looked forward to going home at last for the first time and were yet once again consoled. Important visitors had been announced. Those heroes who had distinguished themselves in the summer battles had been selected to take part in a parade during the visit by the heir to the throne Archduke Karl. It was

Three Kaiserschützen and three Alpini soldiers without their weapons, smiling peacefully into the camera in summer 1916. They simply did not want to carry on fighting. The picture was taken between the Greater and Lesser Eiskögele summits on the Ortler.

whispered to them that this was a special honour. However for the moment they were more interested in finding out how they could get a proper bath, become deloused and be provided with new uniforms and shoes, "for we could hardly face the future Kaiser in our filthy and dishevelled condition." For the first time in ages they felt reborn and were even given brand-new uniforms to replace their ragged ones. The Dolomite mountain guides with ropes over their shoulders and ice axes, the Standschützen, Kaiserjäger and all the others, a motley crowd of men who still bore the burden of the summer battles paraded reverently before the very men who ultimately had a part in sending them to the slaughter.

A man with a peculiar beaver-fur cap caught their eye. When they encountered him again on a woodland walk that afternoon they asked him to show them his papers. "The man smiled and gave us his identity card from which we saw that we were talking to the famous Asia explorer Sven Hedin from Stockholm. He had been given permission from the highest authority at military headquarters to visit all positions and formations." The young students could hardly believe it and bowed reverently before the man whose adventure books they had all read and held in high esteem.

On 5th October 1915 they eventually received the unexpected news that they were to be relieved. At last they could look forward to seeing their families and friends, and a respite from the rigours of the front. Karl Mayr and the few who remained thought once again of their school. They wanted to take their university entrance exams, then to return to the war for the first time as proper soldiers. And so they left behind them an epoch which had changed their lives. An "unkempt, bearded young soldier" returned home and not even his own mother recognised him. The young soldier asked: "'What's wrong? Have I changed so much?' At that she flung her arms around me, cried with joy and kissed me."

His mother made him breakfast and washed her son who was still covered in dirt. Then she let him sleep soundly. When she finally waked him gently he sat up with a start and looked for something which was not there. "I was grasping for my rifle, for in my subconscious I was still serving at the front where, if you are woken suddenly it means reach for your rifle and get ready for action." His relations were also proud of the youngster who had returned alive. An uncle gave him an aluminium and copper ring made from shrapnel. The war had reached even the most remote village and living room. It dominated everyone's thoughts.

Karl Mayr sat his 'Matura' (A-levels) as an eighteen year-old. He was given a choice of two subjects for composition: 'How sweet it is to die for the Fatherland' and 'The exploitation of water power'. "The German master was certain I would choose the former, but I told him 'Sir, I can't because I would have to lie. Believe me, there is nothing sweet about dying for the Fatherland – on the contrary, it is unspeakably bitter." The master was taken aback by this mournful answer and surprised when the young student chose instead the subject dealing with water, steam engines, hydroelectric dams and turbines. The masters despaired of the youth who in the meantime had only learnt one thing: combat – fighting and shooting. They wrung their hands over his lack of the very basics of arithmetic and struggled as hard as they could to coax the little knowledge of mathematics he had out of him. Finally with plenty of good will on all sides the lowly Standschütze Karl Mayr passed his 'Matura'. What he did not manage to do was to get a foothold in normal life.

"A person who at eighteen has looked death in the eye in its multifaceted forms and who, like me has killed people, he has smashed all the conventional ideals of youth. He faces the task of slowly forming new ideals on the broken pieces of the shattered ones, ideals which can then serve as a basis for a later real relationship with life. And so I stood on the cracked plinth of my youthful ideals after passing by exams, ideals which could no longer serve as a foundation for my future life."

Self-doubt wore the young man down. He could no longer grasp the meaning of life. In a time of peace he might have been able to cope, but the war continued with unrelenting ruthlessness without him. "It was war and this was such an all-out war that the civilian sector of the state faded into insignificance." The young Standschütze was overcome with resignation. In his home town he began to search like a maniac for God as a symbol for justice and peace, but found him nowhere. "Like a moloch the war had engulfed everybody and everything including me. Nobody could imagine how anybody swimming in these heavy seas could ever struggle to the shore of a peaceful existence. Neither could religious belief provide me with answers while I was in this state of mind. Where was God and what kind of god would allow thousands upon thousands of those created in His likeness to tear each other apart in the most hideous manner and still pray fervently for Him to grant their side victory and consequently to annihilate the enemy? Why did He remain silent? Had his omnipotence dwindled to the point where he could no longer put an end to this mass slaughter among his own children? After all, according to the Gospel that is what we are. On both sides priests bless the most horrific weapons of mass destruction which human ingenuity had ever produced, and said nothing. Whoever started to think in this way must have begun to doubt the loving kindness, almightiness and justness of this god, while the prayers which an eighteen year-old youth directed at him received no cathartic echo. How welcome it would have been to find a priest or other person who could explain all this and to soothe the restlessness in my tormented heart. To form a clear attitude for the future! But I found none. All those who I knew, even those whose principal task it was to impart the kind of comfort and inner tranquillity to youths maturing into men which they needed to enter adulthood as people of firmly established character with a profoundly-based religious background were blinkered and tediously trotted out the usual platitudes of bourgeois morals and empty phrases."

Karl Mayr was plagued by doubt. Which profession should he choose? He came to grief on himself and the war. His mother noticed his trepidation and tried to console him. "First of all you will have see how you cope with this war as a soldier." She advised him to wait until after the war to decide on a profession. However, an answer presented itself suddenly and spontaneously.

He failed his medical examination – this time for the real army. "First of all I was declared unfit, the reason being that a slight spinal curvature which I had had since my childhood had become aggravated over the past summer to the point where it had somehow affected my heart." He who had braved the inclemencies and vagaries of nature for months on end and who had fought until he was ready to drop was now supposed to be unfit for the army? The valiant soldier became defiant. "If the Fatherland spurns me as an active soldier, I have no desire to continue as a volunteer in the Sandschützen." And he really was given leave. Strangely the Fatherland had no further use for the worthy Standschütze. Defiantly he decided to study law, though the cussedness of the regulations began to harass him. It was true that he had passed his exams, but only as a soldier. The certificate he required to enrol was not issued in spite of vigorous efforts. Nevertheless he wanted to make good use of the time available and attend lectures. The universities were almost empty of male students. There were only female students who struggled on as best they could in those degenerate times of general decay. He began to feel increasingly like a loner, "for I felt rather shy towards the female students, even though hardly any were specimens of feminine beauty, because I had had little experience with girls." Until the professors at Innsbruck University realised that the student Mayr actually had no right to attend their lectures. Politely but firmly they showed him the door. He had become a third class citizen, an alien, beyond the law. A teenager who believed in his Fatherland and had been prepared to lay down his life for it had been rendered superfluous.

"At the time I was completely dissatisfied with my situation and I almost became a misogynist. While the nation's young men were out there on the front armed and fighting for the survival and future of our empire, here was I, spiritually isolated sitting with female swots armed with spectacles."

A new unexpected opportunity presented itself. As if in derision the loyal Standschützen needed him and sent for him because of a dire shortage of manpower. Proudly Karl Mayr declined. The cadre commander explained the situation more bluntly – if he didn't go "then a family head with five children would have to." The lad had no alternative but to accept, to spare an elderly family man such a fate. And so the eighteen year-old who had been declared unfit for military duty had to return to the war once again as a Standschütze.

122

Nothing but mutineers – Today you, tomorrow me – Nothing but dead bodies and more dead bodies – One can't escape one's destiny

On 25th February, 1916 the loyal Standschütze Karl Mayr put on his uniform and made his way to his battalion at Innichen. The Standschützen were called upon to replenish the human material – military jargon for cannon fodder - lost in recent bloody battles. They still resembled a ragged army.

"None of the last year's students were left, but there were several new ones and in addition a few intellectuals who I soon made friends with." The regular troops criticised the Standschützen for being a disorganised unit of volunteers, while yet others denied them any role whatsoever in the fighting. Even the Standschützen themselves had to admit that they comprised for the most part a wild horde of scraggly youths with unorthodox, unmilitary behaviour.

"It was interesting at the time to observe the spirit of our Standschützen. A casual observer would have thought we were all mutineers." They were indifferent to courts martial or military guidelines. They swore and railed against their superiors. "The older Standschützen came almost entirely from the rural community and for them the war was dragging on for far too long. Their folks at home struggled with the upkeep of their farmsteads and fields and still there was no end of this war in sight." But they were still among the comrades who were most willing to go into action selflessly for their home country.

The idyll at Innichen had hardly lasted three days when the alarm was given. They had to move out. Major Hans Fuchs pranced around restlessly with his white horse in the courtyard. They were informed that "something awful had happened in the front sector of Schluderbach". They had to set out as quickly as possible and by evening the entire Standschützen battalion was marching in the direction of the Höhlenstein valley. When they turned off to Landro "a snow storm started which cost the heavily burdened men all the strength they could muster. Our company trudged over knee-deep through the snow which covered the road in drifts with unbelievable speed and the storm howled around our ears filling all with fear and worry. The exhausted troops were hardly given a minute's rest. 'Forwards, keep going' was the order and the major rode the length of the column on his white horse. He made sure that nobody lagged behind, for anybody who did was bound to freeze to death in the awful snow-storm." A severe avalanche disaster had occurred. In spite of the unrelenting, raging snowstorm they struggled on to the mound of avalanche snow in the hope of saving lives. It was only then that they found out about the awful tragedy which had taken place. Three hundred soldiers belonging to the elite Kaiserschützen had marched forward to the Gemärk saddle. At that moment a mass of powder-snow became dislodged from the slopes of the Raukofel, burying the advance party consisting of twenty men. When the troops in the rear rushed to help the most inconceivable thing happened. "A second, far more terrible avalanche thundered down from the slopes of the Raukofel and buried the entire two companies after it had already swept away a sparse forest. This disaster gave rise to an even more perilous situation in as far as it had denuded an entire section of the front of its defenders, with the danger that the Italians could take advantage of the gap and confusion to advance. But thank God this did not happen and although this dreadful avalanche disaster had occurred almost before their eyes they kept calm and fired not a single shot to obstruct the rescue efforts. We knew that Alpine troops or 'Alpini' were among the enemy ranks and these first rate high mountain soldiers who I have already mentioned were acquainted first hand with the devastating power of such natural disasters in the high mountains and were chivalrous enough not to take advantage of our plight. They probably said to themselves 'today you, tomorrow me'." In spite of their exhaustion and the danger of their situation the Standschützen toiled all night in the forlorn hope of finding at least a few of survivors. "They dug just dead bodies and even more dead bodies out of the snow, many of which had been horribly deformed by the trees and rocks which the avalanche had torn from the mountainside. When we moved towards Landro at daybreak to join in the rescue work we saw the dead lying beside the road in long rows. The white death had claimed the lives of over 250 men, 6 officers and a military chaplain. It was a dreadful sight which brought tears to the eyes of even the most hardened men." They only managed to dig thirty soldiers still alive from the stone-hard snow, often using just their bear hands. They were all that remained of the once so proud Kaiserschützen company.

Young Karl Mayr could not help but aim a bitter accusation at the commanders. "Local Standschützen with an intimate knowledge of the terrain would have occasionally warned against such disasters, but at the green tables of the general staff they knew better and catastrophes such as this became inevitable." Those in command took too little notice of the Standschützen who knew their local mountains. Too often they built positions and quarters in summer without considering the conditions which would prevail in winter, close to declivities well-known for being prone to avalanches. Chosen by commanders with only second hand knowledge of life in the mountains.

Unfit for active duty, Standschütze Karl Mayr was assigned to the telephonists, a small exchange with connections to all front positions. "During one of his brief visits to the front the heir to the throne, Archduke Karl entered this telephone exchange hut and asked to speak to the commander of the position on Monte Piano. The telephone operator on Monte Piano enjoyed joking and usually answered calls from his colleagues as the 'Emperor of China'. When the aristocratic visitor rang and gave his name as Archduke Karl the operator on Monte Piano naturally thought that his colleague on the Nasswand was having a laugh and answered promptly as the 'Emperor of China'. He asked jokingly how his 'royal cousin' was faring. Archduke Karl who had a good sense of humour quickly understood the situation and began having a chat with the 'Emperor of China' while those listening were splitting their sides with laughter. The operator on Monte Piano must have had a shock when he found out who he had really been talking to and expected a severe punishment." However the future Kaiser tried to calm things saying that that kind of humour was valuable above all in wartime, that they should leave the 'Emperor of China' alone and under no circumstances punish him.

"Apparently a few days afterwards the operator, who had become almost despondent after the misapprehension, received a box of good cigarettes with a hand-written note from the heir to the throne saying: 'from the cousin of the Emperor of China, Archduke Karl'."

The war days passed. Karl Mayr felt almost unnaturally content, "but in those days a Standschütze arrived among a troop of replacements from home of whom, because of his stylish appearance - he wore a special uniform made of the choicest material - one wondered how he had become a simple member of this Schützen guild. This man was the editor and owner of the book-printing company Ferdinand Zelenka, a man aged around forty with the appearance of an intellectual. He was immediately assigned to my job in the battalion office and I was 'demoted' to the position of telephone orderly."

All of a sudden this man was to change Karl Mayr's life. For although the young Standschütze was angry, Zelenka immediately won his friendship. He advised him to be prudent and asked Karl to trust him, saying he was in a position to enrich his life. And Karl Mayr instinctively discerned the great power of the older Standschütze's superiority and wisdom. Their common destiny was to bind them increasingly closer together.

"Ferdinand Zelenka was not only a man with immense universal knowledge, but was also a rich man by the standards of the time, who moved in the best social circles. His wife with whom he had enjoyed an ideal marriage was a close relation of the Nordic poet Knud Hamsun but she had died shortly before he joined up. He must have adored this woman for when she died he abandoned everything and joined up as a simple Standschütze just to forget. He wanted to get over the dolour he suffered at the loss of his wife in a completely different milieu and for this reason he turned up unexpectedly among us. This was even more surprising given that in his general ideology Zelenka was a resolute pacifist who viewed this war and its effects from a loftier standpoint than I did. I discussed this subject with him often over the following weeks and it gradually dawned on me that things would turn out the way he predicted. He did not think that we would win this war because all aspects of the political developments in European countries and above all those in America stacked the odds against us. When I asked him why he had put on the uniform under such auspices he shrugged his shoulders and said: 'One can't escape one's own destiny and perhaps I have taken my fate by the horns. For the individual this is often more likely to lead to a solution than does persisting as a pacifist'."

"I profited much from this man in yet another aspect. Soldiers and also comrades given the right situation would often discuss sexual subjects among themselves, often in very candid terms. Not least among them was my friend the medical student Wurnig who could describe scenes which, to put it mildly, could not be repeated in the company of ladies. So much emphasis was placed purely on the physical side of love in such talk that a young, innocent man like I was then became tempted to get the completely wrong impression of love. Then time and time again it fell to my friend Zelenka to put a due damper on this dissolute talk by stressing with his convincing force of personality that all what was said was well and good but was not the true essence of love. Rather it depleted the spiritual relationship between man and wife and love could only attain the peak where it produced mutual happiness for two persons within the framework of such a relationship. It was not the sexual act which contained the essence of love, but rather the developments leading to it. He never hesitated to explain and prove the soundness of this view based on the nature of his own marriage. "Love, my dear friends", he would often say, "it is like a difficult musical instrument which one has to learn to play. Many never learn it at all, pluck the strings with rough, awkward fingers and produce nothing but discords. Others learn it only like amateurish dilettanti and consequently their love play cannot not satisfy either. Few become genuine masters on this instrument but the notes they coax from it produce heavenly music." Karl Mayr began to admire Zelenka and his manner. He was worldly-wise and of high intellect, a person who one simply had to respect.

A singular occurrence in the history of this wretched war – No patriotism can justify these dead – Let those down below carry on the war! – We are making peace

Monte Piana (2,325m) and Monte Piano (2,305m) are two summits which form a plateau along an extensive ridge above the narrow Höhlenstein (Landro) valley. Together with Monte Piana, the Raukofel guarded the entrance to the Höhlenstein valley and was firmly under Tyrolean control. However in a surprise attack during the night between 31st March and 1st April 1916 700 experienced Italian Alpine troops managed to take the summit. Although the Austrian howitzer batteries fired continuously at the Rauhkofel from the Schönleiten gap with such intensity that the gunners received burn wounds to their hands and had to use snow to cool the almost red hot barrels of their cannons, the valiant Alpinis held on tenaciously and all attempts to retake the mountain failed with heavy losses. Then in a masterstroke two heavy machine guns were hauled up a three-hundred metre high icy rock face to the Schönleiten-Spitze and began to fire more effectively on the courageous Italians. Finally after a ferocious six-day battle the Austrians retook the summit where, of the 700 Italian Alpine troops only 90 were still alive and many of those were badly wounded. A completely haggard group of soldiers, hollow-eyed from the strain was led hobbling and bound with all kinds of bandages into the Nasswand camp. And then something happened which the Young Tyrolean Standschütze described as "A singular occurrence in the history of this wretched war":

"As the captured Italians limped along the road through the camp they were scoffed at and almost attacked by members of the Ruthenian territorial army, those pitiful characters who had distinguished themselves so ingloriously. At that point the Nasswand camp commander (Kaiserschützen-Major Fuchs) intervened in a way which recalled the chivalry of centuries long past. He bade the Italian prisoners to stop. He then ordered the Rutherian soldiers to line up beside the road in full battle dress and salute the Italians as they walked past. At first the Italians were confused and looked with intimidated expressions at the troops who were saluting them. However once they realised what was happening an Italian lieutenant with a blood-soaked bandage around his head suddenly stepped out of the column, walked up to Major Fuchs and shook his hand saying simply: 'Grazie, tante grazie!' (Thank you, many thanks)." Even Karl Mayr was overwhelmed with emotion at that scene.

"It is a great pity that the grand, heroic event could not be captured in a photograph, for it would have served as a monument to the greatness of humanity."

Alas! Pictures of such moments showing genuine human dignity cannot exist, for if such a war photo did it could be conducive to avoiding future conflicts and would be suppressed. It would be destroyed and the author cursed. How easy it is to take photographs – often posed - of artillery, or groups of heavily armed men and how much more difficult it is to capture moments of humanity in war. "It was then that the awful tragedy of war and the insanity of this self-laceration of men first came home to me. My friend Zelenka was right when he said: 'No patriotism can justify or excuse this slaughter'."

After these battles which claimed thousands of dead the "stiffly frozen bodies were slid down over rocks and precipitous snow-covered meadows like logs" during the following nights and buried. It sounded far more prosaic in the general staff report of 8th April 1916: "The battles for the Rauhkofl were completed victoriously with the recapture of the mountain." It contains not a trace of how things really were, not a line about the scene of respect, mutual admiration and peace which took place at the meeting of the downtrodden troops. War always takes place where there is no truth.

"I would like to mention another episode from these winter and spring battles in this part of the Dolomite front which added a more personal touch to events and of which my friend Zelenka remarked with shining eyes that the world would be a much better place if we all behaved like this. I mention the occurrence not only because of its unusual nature, but also because I doubt whether it has been mentioned anywhere in the annals of the First World War. The episode could be called the 'peace settlement on the Schönleiten-Spitze' and this is how it happened:

"The Schönleiten-Spitze is a 2,722 metre high summit in the lower elevations of the Monte Cristallo massif, completely isolated, cut-off and inaccessible in winter. A platoon of Kaiserjäger troops of around 40 men under the command of a lieutenant was positioned there. A group of Italian Alpine troops of the same strength was situated on the southern lower summit ridge around 50 paces from our own position. Throughout the summer months of 1915 these two groups waged war against each other as they were supposed to. However when winter threatened – as it did up there as early as October – their provisions for the whole winter were quickly supplied to them, after which they were left to their own fates, for after the first heavy snowfall in November they could not be re-supplied.

"It is clear to everybody that the winter months on the Schönleiten-Spitze was no bed of roses, alone because of the struggle against the elements. Forty men who lived there in a makeshift hut had to fend entirely for themselves and could not expect help from anywhere. It was up to them to manage to live through the winter months. Given that the Italians on the lower summit ridge fared little better it was tacitly agreed that the two groups would not shoot at each other. To what purpose? There would have been no point, for both sides needed all the energy they could muster to prevail against the powers of nature, the storms and bitter cold. Things continued as normal until February 1916, when both sides realised that certain supplies were getting so short that they were seriously worried whether they could hold out until spring. It happened that an Italian guard called across to our men – they were only 50 paces apart – saying that they had run out of tobacco and could our men spare some. After asking around our guard answered that they had plenty of tobacco but were running out of fuel. At this one of the sides suggested a ceasefire and that they should help each other out. The commanders of both sides agreed and upon meeting they discovered that it would not be unthinkable for the Italians to supply our men with fuel in exchange for tobacco. This exchange and bartering was subsequently extended to various foodstuffs, for it turned out that the Italians still had plentiful supplies of rice, of which they would gladly exchange a few bags for our side's dried vegetables. Both sides, both ours and the Italians, came to realise that the enemy consisted of rather nice men and, given that both sides were engaged in the same bitter fight against the pitiless forces of nature a certain human mountain comradeship developed which took the form of both sides saying: 'Let them make war down there in the valley! Up here we haven't the slightest inclination to smash each others' heads in and riddle each other with bullets. We are making peace and intend to keep it as long as the others let us.'

"It came about naturally that our men were invited to the Italian positions and they to ours. Scenes of fraternisation took place, with spirits lubricated with Italian wine and Austrian schnapps and rum. In short, up on the Schönleiten-Spitze peace was realised in the winter months of a kind which hundreds of soldiers down in the valley on both sides longed for with every fibre of their being but could not bring about because leaders and diplomats of the various nations simply did not want it.

"This truce on the Schönleiten-Spitze lasted well as long as the soldiers were cut off from the rest of mankind, though the situation became critical in April 1916 when normal communications with the valley began to be established. The commander of the Austrian troops began to feel uneasy about the consequences and the Italian commander probably felt the same. Out of necessity the men began to separate and return to their positions. They did not fire on each other, but the front was restored. There was a sequel to this episode, conducted before a court martial. This 'peace' on the Schönleiten-Spitze could not be kept a secret and the platoon was consequently relieved. The commander had to explain himself before the military divisional court and the commander of the Italian occupants of this mountain probably fared little better. I have no idea about the outcome of the court martial case. I heard nothing more about it."

The grim reaper wielded his scythe unabated – Solemnly they sang the Lord's Prayer – Emperor Karl was a man too weak for such hard times - A medal for bravery does not constitute a hero

The Dolomites were just a small island in the general slaughter and bloodbath. From April 1916 all forces were concentrated in the Val-Sugana valley connecting Trento with the Veneto plain in order to penetrate through to the flatland in the area of Padua and Venice and drive a wedge between the Italian armies and the front on the Isonzo river. However the weather proved unfavourable while at the same time the Russian General Brussilow launched an even more vehement attack against the Austrian 4th army on Austria's northeastern frontier in the province known then as Galicia, which today straddles the border between Poland and the Ukraine. Units were hurriedly dispatched from the Dolomites to the eastern front to replenish the depleted positions with fresh cannon fodder in order to avert an impending disaster. "In the mean time the Grim Reaper wielded his scythe relentlessly on the Isonzo and claimed hecatombs of lives on both sides. One Isonzo attack after another was beaten back as the Italians endeavoured with all available forces to break through to Trieste. They failed. Our front on the Isonzo weakened a little, but held, while the Italians had to pay for a gain of just 2 km of terrain with ten thousand dead."

For the time being Karl Mayr enjoyed a period of calm. He had been used to bearing responsibility on the front line and now felt out of his element as a telephone operator. At least he had time to read and further his studies in peace and quiet.

"At that time and afterwards news from home was far from cheering. My stepfather was suspended from duty because of a malicious calumny and was summoned before a court martial accused of irredentist activities which by then were considered high treason. After a lengthy trial during which he was even kept in custody he was eventually found not guilty. However he was no longer admitted to return to service but had to join the army where, notwithstanding his civilian position and previous training as a regular soldier, he was drafted to the railway and telegraph regiment." He was transferred to the front where he was bullied and robbed of his human dignity.

Karl Mayr grew more mature by the day. He was observant, wanted to learn and become a respectable person. At that time Russian prisoners of war were being deployed to build a road in the Höhlenstein (Landro) valley. They were badly treated and badly fed. They were for the most part older men and were given a meal of maize porridge only once a day at noon. And even though Karl Mayr knew that this was too little by far considering their strenuous work, he was surprised at their gestures of brotherliness. "They formed a ring around the cauldron of porridge, took off their hats and sang the Lord's Prayer in their Russian mother tongue. They sang it so beautifully and rousingly in harmony with deep bass tones and joyful tenor voices that I could not help but listen and was deeply moved. What profound belief could have moved these simple Russian POWs to thank God with such intensity for a meal which far more resembled pig swill?"

News also arrived from the home front. In those fateful days the emperor, Kaiser Franz Josef, died in Schönbrunn palace in Vienna, "after he had put his signature to his last documents the day before with a hand trembling with fever. With him died the last real emperor of the Old World, for his successor, Kaiser Karl, was no longer capable of bearing the burden of an Austrian emperorship which destiny had imposed on him, but could only fall with the monarchy." The inexorable downfall continued. "As a ruler his successor, Emperor Karl, to whom we soldiers immediately had to swear allegiance, lacked the charisma and

130

outstanding personality of his father. He was the last person who could have averted the looming disaster which was to accompany the downfall of a state. He may have been a man of good intentions with many other laudable qualities which up to then had stood him in good stead as successor to the throne and as commander of the armed forces and gained him a certain popularity among the soldiers. But in the final analysis he was too soft and weak for such hard times. Towards the end when it gradually emerged that he stood completely under the influence of his domineering consort, the Bourbon princess Zita, he even lost the dwindling support of his subject nations which the old Kaiser Franz Joseph had still managed to retain in spite of their centrifugal nationalistic tendencies."

Each side tried to outdo the other with new technology. Incessant shelling by the Italians on Monte Piano claimed countless deaths among the Standschützen battalions. In contrast with the shells which only blasted large craters in the ground, when the galleries dug beneath the opposing positions and filled with explosives were detonated the explosion caused devastation in all directions. Alone the rush of air generated by the explosion caused huts to collapse and soldiers to die the most agonising death.

The oldest among us, Ferdinand Zelenka, gained the respect of all and became unofficially looked upon as our leader. One of the reasons was the remarkable way how, in all situations, he could adapt to younger troops who were mostly his intellectual inferiors. He tried to help them with their problems whenever he could. For example when Karl Mayr's friend Sieberer showed him a forces' mail service letter written by a third company Standschütze to his wife:

"My darling little spouse! I heard from Simmerl Leitner who was recently home on leave that you're having an affair with our neighbour Lois. Dear me, you can both look forward to my homecoming! There won't be much left of Lois and you won't get over the thrashing that's coming to you in a hurry. Apart from that I send you my best wishes. Your ever-loving husband Franz." Love and faithfulness in marriage were always among the first victims in war. If one wanted to survive the present day the last thing one ought to think of was the tomorrow.

The Italians began once again to shell Toblach vehemently from Cortina d'Ampezzo. The aim was to put the railway out of service. Although no trains were hit the tracks were badly damaged as well as many of the magnificent hotels which a few years earlier had boasted Europe's aristocracy among their guests. There were no fatalities apart from those caused by youthful recklessness, when teenage boys tried to hammer the copper guide ring off of a stray shell, which exploded and blew the unfortunate boys to pieces." Still the inhabitants of Toblach carried on as normal and "it was amazing how calmly the farmers went about their work in the fields even though they were hardly 200 metres from the target area."

Karl Mayr also received his first war decoration, the 'Karl Truppenkreuz' or 'Karl Troop Cross', awarded to all troops including militias who had served at least 12 weeks on the front and who had participated in at least one battle. He had expected a higher distinction but reacted sarcastically, "that a bravery medal has not always denoted a genuine hero." In September 1916 the Italian artillery intensified its bombardment of the villages Toblach, Niederdorf, Innichen and Sillian, while the Austrians in retaliation bombarded Cortina. Nevertheless the general situation became calmer. Stalemate had ensued on all fronts, the positions had been so well fortified that they had become unassailable bulwarks. Besides, nobody was particularly interested in provoking the other side. Everywhere networks of galleries had been excavated which served as supply tunnels. Both sides tried to blow up individual enemy positions though neither this stratagem led to the desired outcome. In the meantime almost all positions in the high mountains had been connected by an extensive network of telephone lines and some quarters even had electric lighting. Consequently "the war became veritable siege warfare in which the balance between the opposing forces no longer produced surprises, particularly since we all knew that events on our front would hardly determine the real outcome of this war."

It snowed incessantly day and night – Four metres of snow – Peace on earth to all men – God works no wonders at the request of us small humans

The warm months of 1916 passed and men were already preparing for the coming winter. They anticipated it reassured, thinking they had learnt the necessary lessons from the last season and confident that the positions and supply lines were protected from avalanches. The 20th October still brought glorious sunny autumn weather. "Then one afternoon around 24th October the sky suddenly darkened, dusk came early, it became cold and the first snowflakes wafted down from the skies. Initially they were just individual snowflakes, but then the snowfall became more intense and the following night it snowed like I had never seen before. An increasingly thicker mist of unusually large snowflakes descended upon the surroundings. It snowed incessantly all night long and when the wan daybreak revealed the forests, mountains and meadows mantled in white the snow continued to fall with unabated intensity and did not let up the entire following night. When the snowfall relented at least for intervals on the third day we found ourselves under some three metres of snow." Then the struggle began against hostile nature, which brought everything to a halt. However this only provided a wretched breathing space, for the snowfall resumed with an intensity never seen before. The huts were soon buried beneath metres-high walls of snow. Men battled their way through the snow on rackets or on skis.

"Hundreds of Russian prisoners of war were deployed to keep the Dolomite roads clear for traffic, but with only partial success. Once the snow depth exceeded four metres it became impossible to clear it from the road. What next? The only solution was to dig tunnels. By Christmas 1916 all traffic from the Nasswand to the frontline positions passed through tunnels in the snow." Hundreds of prisoners of war somehow managed to keep road as far as the Nasswand camp in the Höhlenstein (Landro) valley accessible though men had to struggle between walls of snow several metres high. In the face of mortal danger soldiers had to keep the troops who were holding out in the high mountains supplied with provisions. "The heavy horses in our column were unable to cope with the fatigue and almost all died. Only the mules and the tough, stalwart Hucul (Carpathian) horses managed to withstand the rigours."

Life on the front became quiet. "Not even the artillery fired another shot, for the shells mostly thudded into the snow as duds. The personnel lay snowed-in down below throughout the winter and killed the time with sleeping and playing cards." Quiet and peace prevailed everywhere, quietude which both sides welcomed. And not even the avalanches caused such horrendous havoc as in the previous winter.

"There was the occasional avalanche during the winter months but men had gained experience during the last winter, were on their guard and no significant accidents occurred. One small avalanche near the Katzenleiter hit an Italian trench position and tore several Alpinis down into our own trenches, where they were greeted by our smiling soldiers."

Christmas was approaching for the second time, although all felt as though the war had already lasted for an eternity. "The men had stuck small Christmas trees decorated with tinsel on several sleighs to remind us that the Saviour was born 1916 years ago in Bethlehem and that the angels had sung 'Peace on earth, good will to all men'. But was that really peace? Peace still seemed distant, so distant that we had reached the point where we could no longer believe in it." On that 24th December, 1916 the young Standschütze drowned his despair in wine. "We drank wine, plenty of wine, for the soldiers all had money and obviously wanted to forget their sorrows on this Christmas Eve."

The year 1917 began, the fourth war year. The powers-that-were did all they could to replenish the constantly decimated troops. "They succeeded mainly because many eighteen-year-olds in our companies' wards who, on the results of their medicals should have been called up for active service, preferred to join the Standschützen before they had come of age. There they would be under the command of officers who they knew from their home areas, also the training and discipline were less rigorous compared with the active army. In this way our ranks were filled with younger fighting troops, for very few of the older generation were left."

A last-ditch contingent of children was thrown into the conflict. Bad news arrived from all sides. The United States entered the war. Abysmal resignation spread everywhere. The stranglehold of the blockade had already caused shortages. New military innovations caused destruction on industrial scales never seen before. War in the air became the latest neology, armoured vehicles – tanks – were employed for the first time in France. Even the highest forms of gallantry had become outdated. Poison gas attacks added a further horrific dimension to the war. "With a good gasmask and knowledge of how to use it one could defend oneself against attacks with the so-called asphyxiant 'blue-cross' and 'green-cross' gases, though there was no mask could protect against 'yellow-cross' mustard gas, which entered the body through pores tormenting men to death in the most agonising way."

Still a macabre optimism and confidence in victory prevailed somewhere far remote from the simple, exhausted and emaciated troops. "With misguided optimism the New Year 1917 was celebrated in the officers' messes in command posts as the year of final victory and was toasted with wine and liqueurs. We simple soldiers were no longer so certain of victory insofar as we had at our disposal the necessary intelligence and the faculty of logical thought." And even his friend Zelenka put forward his opinion "with unrelenting clarity: 'We have already lost this war'." Even if generals and commanders still wanted to send thousands of men to their deaths, beneath the surface a new world was gradually opening. "I wanted to believe in a miracle which could perhaps work out in our favour, but Zelenka dismissed it with the words: 'God performs no miracles at the request of small people like us'." Each had to bear the yoke of the war in his own way. Some did so with deadened apathy, while others lived each day like animals as if the end of the world was nigh.

Our family was completely torn apart – We would become new persons – That was not an emperor, but a drunkard – There you saw the abominations of hell

Karl Mayr was redeployed to the place where he had undergone the transformation from child to manhood. He was deployed once again to the Kreuzberg pass. As if in derision several of his own 'rolling bombs' of two years before were still lying around rusting. "These giant, black monsters were hollow iron balls filled with explosives, intended to be rolled down the mountainside against an advancing enemy. None of us actually knew how the explosive charge was supposed to be detonated. Anyhow, they were never actually used." He still remembered the Seikofl fortification from 1915 when bloody battles raged there.

And even then the Italian trenches were still only forty paces away. "In this fox-hole with the well-tended grave of an unknown Italian soldier behind, it was not advisable to expose oneself without good covering fire for fear of attracting a well-aimed bullet of an enemy sniper. But perhaps the position was relatively safe precisely for that reason, for both sides saw an advantage in not harassing each other."

He still found the signs of death from the year 1915. "It was precisely in this area that I found a perfectly preserved human skull in the summer of the same year and took it home for my brother to help him in his medicine studies." The war had desensitised everyone. Occurrences which would at one time have stirred the soul were by then mere events which hardly moved anyone anymore. "Enemy deserters came over to us two or three times, showing that the fighting

Museo della Grande Guerra - Passo Fedaia

An act of humanity: A Tyrolean Standschütze carries a wounded Italian soldier to the field hospital.

Sorelle Apollonio

The epitome of peace. An Italian Alpini soldier with a local girl. The cat clings to the girl's dress, while the soldier looks gravely into the camera lost in thought.

morale among the Italians was not exactly at its best and that they themselves had had enough of war, though these were hardly important occurrences which in any way interfered with the normal routine of duty."

Spring arrived once again on the flat, rocky summit of the Seikofel overlooking the Sexten valley. The soldiers passed the time improving their defences. Things were no longer as they had been at the beginning of the war when the men had to dig themselves into the clay to feel reasonably safe. Summer came and the Italians positioned nearby were likewise suffering from combat fatigue. Finally the situation changed dramatically in October 1917. "A storm broke out over our enemy on the front along the Isonzo river in the vicinity of Tolmein/Tolmezzo which turned out to be a rout and a disaster for them." With Russia heading towards civil war and faced with the risk of losing their main ally, Austria, the German high command had decided to send a few divisions to the southern front for a few months. Seven German and eight Austrian divisions under the command of the German general Otto von Bellow achieved an unexpected breakthrough at Caporetto (or Karfreit as it was known to the Central Powers, now Kobarid in Slovenia). Italian losses were breathtaking, with 40,000 dead and wounded, 280,000 taken prisoner – often without fighting because they had been instructed to await orders to attack which never came - and over 400,000 civilian refugees. Two-thirds of the Italian army's artillery pieces plus thousands of machine guns and mortars were also captured. The Austrians everywhere became reinvigorated which renewed confidence in victory. The Italian troops retreated hastily from Schluderbach and Cortina, on the Kreuzberg pass they blew up their remaining ammunition dump and left the theatre without a fight, exhausted and demoralised. However the food rations they left behind were like gourmet delicacies for the hungry Standschützen and Kaiserjäger soldiers.

"An enormous Italian wine store was discovered to the south of Padola and during the plunder by soldiers belonging to the so-called Tranchom battalion – a punitive platoon of our army – several soldiers literally drowned in wine. A giant cask in this store was brought out onto the road and every soldier who passed by on his way north or south was allowed to tap a rations-bowl full. After three weeks the cask was apparently not yet empty.

"On the other hand our soldiers also told of other less pleasant occurrences. The inhabitants of the upper Comelico valley had probably been entirely evacuated earlier, leaving all the villages and farmsteads deserted and empty. Although the Italians had retreated suddenly and in a hurry they had set up plenty of booby traps which, at least initially, claimed casualties among our men. They had also poisoned foodstuffs and in addition, soon afterwards it was discovered by accident that the enemy had filled stoves in private houses with dynamite, leading to further losses when soldiers tried to light them for heating. We soon learnt to be careful on opening doors because in many cases the retreating enemy had attached hand grenades to the door handles with string. As soon as the door was opened the hand grenade exploded."

However the hope that the Italians had been defeated soon proved illusory. It turned out to be a last gleam of hope before the final downfall. Karl Mayr asked his friend Ferdinand Zelenka once again for advice and asked him how he foresaw the end. He auspicated with convincing certainty:

"How should it end? If nothing exceptional happens and the war ends prematurely it will finish in the same way that the scattered Alpini troops on the Elferkofl and on the Monte Cristallo finished up. They carried on fighting a losing battle until, exhausted by hunger they became physically incapable of carrying on. That's how we'll end up." Karl Mayr could do nothing but tacitly agree. He had become a realist and thick-skinned. The final, difficult stage lay ahead and in spite of all reports of victory there was no escaping it. Once again the last reserves were mustered, even his younger brother Artur was called up for service in autumn 1917. By the third day he had contracted pneumonia and was moved from one hospital to another with an infected lung. His stepfather was sent to the front in Val Sugana where he was burdened with the toughest duties and had to endure harsh fatigue. His mother stayed at home and like many others hoped each day that the postman would spare her from bad news. Rural areas became increasingly tormented by hunger.

Karl Mayr received a letter from his stepfather in late autumn 1917 which had for some reason found its way past the censors: "Dear Karl, it is not the war and its immediate effects which make me depressed, but its consequences which I can already discern. Even our family has been completely torn apart and can never again live together in peace and tranquillity the way we used to. And even if we get back together, and please God we will, we will have changed and I am not sure whether we can ever again rediscover the basis for the kind of harmonious family life we once had. Now thousands of families are in the same situation. I dread the future."

Karl Mayr was made to remain on the Seikofl for a considerable time. They could find no proper use for this man who was officially unfit for active service but who had always been ready to do his duty as a loyal soldier. "Our battalion remained on the Seikofl until around the 6th November, when we were withdrawn into the Pustertal valley. There we began a seemingly senseless peregrination. The high command obviously had no idea how to deploy us for, according to regulations, officially we were only allowed to be used to defend the frontiers of Tyrol." Some of his comrades hoped that they would at last be demobilised and set free, but were to be disappointed. The faltering, dying fatherland had not yet claimed enough human victims. The war had to be pursued. To the bitter end.

For the time being they were ordered to march to the village of Sillian in East Tyrol to help with the snow-clearing work. Winter had once again arrived and once again walls of snow towered metres-high. Twenty of them slept together in the cold general room of an inn. They lit the old farmhouse stove with wood to keep warm and before they went to sleep they laid their wet socks and foot rags on top of it. "I was so tired that I fell asleep almost immediately and while I was sleeping I had the sensation subconsciously to be coughing heavily. We were suddenly woken in the middle of the night. Our NCO stood in the doorway with a lantern and shouted: 'Get up men! You'll suffocate in there!' The room was filled with smoke and all were threatened with suffocation. The socks had begun to smoulder."

They were then transferred to Innichen from where they were to be sent to an uncertain destination on the front. Then they were subsequently sent by train to Trento. He looked on with incredulity as a long column of Italian prisoners of war who had been captured fighting on the Asiago high plateau were flood-lit in the Piazza d'Armi square in Trento. "What a haunting spectacle of war", a sight which, like many others, left a lasting impression on him.

There was also another episode he would never forget. "It was a pathetic parade which shocked even us. 'Is that an emperor?' we asked ourselves. What had happened to the cheerful, radiant Archduke Karl of the year 1915? The Kaiser was quite obviously drunk. Red in the face, he staggered from one division to another, slurred his speech, toadied up to the columns of soldiers standing to attention and was continuously moved on by his retinue. The black sinister-looking figure of his domineering consort, Empress Zita Bourbon-Parma, walked beside him. She seemed to us like a wicked angel. The parade was cut short because the emperor had supposedly become unwell. There were several old Standschützen among us after the parade, war veterans who literally cried and said: 'What are we supposed to do with this Kaiser? He's not an emperor, just a man who gets drunk to escape misery!'" The same emperor who the Vatican proclaimed 'Blessed' in 2004 and who is on the road to sainthood because of his virtuousness. Which makes a mockery of all the men who were sent to their deaths. The creeping decline and fall became more and more obvious. Even though everyone still tried to embrace all the sensuous pleasures of life with open arms. "In the evening certain Standschützen said they were going to the 'Castell Links'. That was the official soldiers' brothel in Trento. My friend Ferdinand Zelenka said to me: 'Come on, let's go too!'

"I was scandalised and asked if he had no conscience or self-respect to even think of such a thing. However my friend, the experienced man of the world smiled.

"'You misunderstand me. I don't want to take you there for you to indulge yourself, but for you to look into an abyss and free yourself for ever from this kind of poison called sex'. I really did look into an abyss of moral depravity from which I recoiled with a shudder. I was spared the description of the atrocious milieu of this anteroom of venal love. My friend Zelenka seemed to me like the mentor Virgil who guided Dante through hell. He whispered to me:

"'You are still an innocent, uncorrupted young man who dreams of fine ideals. I have showed you this so that you remain so and recognise the kind of love you should not aspire to. Love can be heaven or hell. Here you can see hell, ugly, abominable hell. Real, true love, my friend, can only unfold in aesthetics and beauty, and only people who understand how to preserve human dignity in sexual matters can enjoy the true fruits of love. Remember that for the rest of your life!'

"Without a word I squeezed my friend's hand and we left that place of iniquity."

Like vagrants from a long gone era they had to continue their march from Trento to the lakes of Garda and Toblino. They still carried their winter coats from the Dolomites, though one after another they discarded their winter clothing and equipment which by then had become useless. Until even the last Standschütze who was still carrying his skis flung them angrily into the lake in a wide spread. Even he felt that the time had come when he would no longer need them. A military band came towards them once again when they entered the village of Dro wearing their dilapidated uniforms. As the battalion of pathetic figures marched into the village they struck up a Tyrolean march on their instruments which were painted in field grey. They were cheered and praised as heroes. They were welcomed by a general who extolled them courteously and asked if they had any requests. One of the older Standschützen blurted out that he was starving. The general dismissed this complaint with a curse saying that he could do nothing about food and that he himself had already endured several days there with an empty stomach. And so they consoled each other that at least where they were the sun provided soothing warmth.

Food rations became even more meagre and scarce, the twenty grams of bread no longer sufficed even for breakfast. Necessity is the mother of invention. "Our men were far from indolent in these matters and from time to time resorted to self-help. For example, what was the purpose of all those well-fed cats which roamed around the village? I too ate cat meat several times in those days and have to admit that it tasted superb. In our ground-floor kitchen a fat tomcat, sizzled in a pan with hard-to-procure potatoes was like a gala dinner for us four house occupants."

Karl Mayr began to meditate even more about the fair sex. "It was extremely difficult to puzzle out whether the numerous young girls in the village – some of whom were incredibly pretty – were camp followers or just innocent village girls." Until after long reflection he came to the cynical conclusion, "that these wenches must have had something to do with the military, for they could not have lived from what they had." And so in the face of the inevitable destiny the final flakes of pure innocence gradually crumbled from the virtuous Standschütze Mayr who by then was already twenty years old

I cared nothing more for the war – Let them cope without me – Now we have lost everything – Nobody can rob us of our homeland, its valleys, mountains and forests

Christmas 1917 hurried towards its end. Things were even more desperate than they had been the preceding year. Standschütze Karl Mayr was granted home leave to sit some university exams. A Red Cross sister took pity on him and darned his trousers as best she could before he was permitted to return home after such a long absence. "It's not exactly perfect, but it's the best I can do", she remarked looking at his worn-out uniform full of holes. However this no longer bothered Karl Mayr. He had long taken his leave from all this. That country, that life, that war. He could only answer the nonplussed nurse with "I'll only throw them to the rags anyhow." Still, he thanked her warmly for her help.

Over the years Karl Mayr had learnt to see through the various press releases. "Successful defensive battles in France …. victorious battles on the Italian front, massive sinking of shipping tonnage by our submarines and pretentious reports about the riches of the Ukraine which were now ours but of which we noticed nothing." The stalwart soldier had matured and become wiser. He simply no longer wanted to fight. Not only he. But still his fatherland reached out for him, the official cripple, like a moloch. He was called once again to the front. But no sense of idealism, no love of the fatherland, no pleading appeal from the war lords could bring him to return. "I no longer cared for the war and its occurrences. Let them cope without me, for I could no longer be saddled with someone else's causes, help pull the cart out of mire into which it was constantly sinking further."

Mayr the upright Standschütze had learnt too much during these war years. He had learnt to see through the commanders, the heartlessness of the powerful, the moving around of ordinary men like pawns in a game. His wounded soul was sick and he had turned it inside-out. He rejected the war and not even the most emotional appeal could change his mind. He was intent on saving his own selfhood from this slough of futility by whatever means. As an observer of a dying era he saw the 'white censured spaces' in the newspapers becoming larger and larger. News about mutineering troops reached even the smallest Tyrolean villages. The old empire was dying and its various ethnic groups wanted to decide freely which nation to give their allegiance. The months – September,

October - passed agonisingly. On 2nd November 1918 Tyrol became filled with soldiers fleeing home from the front. "Each just wanted to return home and was anxious to do so as quickly as possible. The national roads abounded with single soldiers and groups of soldiers who seemed to be wandering aimlessly. The prisoner of war camps had also emptied and everyone who emerged simply wanted to head for home."

They were like doddery skeletons and even the horses were rawboned and starving. They were slaughtered and the meagre meat distributed among the equally hungry populace, for they could serve no further purpose in the war. On one of the last fine days in November Karl Mayr stood high above the Inn valley with his brother Artur who had long been rejected for military service because of severe pneumonia. They looked across at the mountains of their homeland which Karl had so long believed in.

"In a melancholic undertone my brother said:

'Now the war is over. We've lost everything'.

I was more optimistic and answered:

'Everything? Why everything? Our homeland, the valleys, the mountains, the forests, the blue sky – they've stayed the same, haven't they? Nobody can take them away from us. The people too are still the same spiritually and mentally. In the long run it finally depends on how to reorganise these people on a national basis.'

'That's true of course' remarked my brother, 'but don't forget that the finest of us lay out there dead on the battlefield and that today the dregs of society which remain are the ones which have risen to the top.'

I said nothing. He was right. But finally I said with a deep sigh: 'I can't believe that that's the end. I'm sure life will become more vigorous and, after all, the two of us are still alive!'"

Other occurrences – We broke our weapons – Insights and experience which no school can teach you

What else happened! "Hansl Sieberer, the student from Volders was a good-natured person whose task was to censure and deal with the forces' mail, an assignment which he carried out with plenty of humour". Throughout the war he had remained a good comrade of Karl Mayr's. After the war he continued his medical studies and as "he happened to be examining his own sputum during microscopical exercises he found it to be full of tuberculosis bacilli. A galloping tuberculosis infection broke out in his larynx and he died in autumn 1921."

The world also fell apart for Major Hans Fuchs, the painter who embellished countless churches in Tyrol with his frescoes. During the retreat from Trento into the Sarca valley in November 1918 his battalion was captured. Fuchs "was said to have sat on a rock and cried like a child after giving his final order to his men to smash their weapons and throw them down into the gorge." That stocky man almost sixty years old with his greying beard could not believe it. He, who, was "basically a soft-hearted man and above all I would almost say, a Tyrolean with the naïve piety of a patriarch."

That was the fate of the Standschützen battalion from Hall on the outskirts of Innsbruck, whose men set out in a quest for peace in a war of atrocities. And in the course of these few years the eighteen year-old Standschütze Karl Mayr learnt the "science of insight into human nature, knowledge which no school or university can teach but which I regard as immeasurably more important for the development of an individual's character than knowledge of logarithms or the history of the 30 Year War."

Michael Wachtler

When Austrians, Tyroleans, Italians and Russians celebrated peace. One day during the First World War the soldiers in the Adamello area decided to fight no longer and simply to relax together. They forgot that they were at war.

Paolo Giacomel

Cortina d'Ampezzo 1915. 'Pace' ('peace') is written on this sign held by an 'Angel of Peace'. The war rages in Galicia (eastern Europe), though in spite of the horrific news from the front ordinary people still hope for peace. They have no idea that they will soon find themselves in the midst of the combat area.

Museo Grande Guerra, Ternù

The picture of war. Austrian soldiers with their sweethearts. The photo is torn by a bullet hole bottom left. Italian soldiers found it in a dead Austrian officer's breast pocket.

Sorelle Apollonio

Two Landesschützen medical orderlies, recognisable by their red cross bands, help several Italian soldiers who are lying on the ground wounded. It is precisely scenes such as this depicting willingness to help each other regardless of nationality that are the most moving.

War in Glacier Ice

For the first time occurrences here were shown to the general public through the photographic diary kept by Fritz Malcher, an architect from Baden near Vienna. Day by day he documented events on the Marmolada front, capturing them on fragile glass lantern-slides which were still in use at the time. The development of the war could hardly have been represented more forcefully. Malcher captures the leisurely atmosphere of the first months and how, from the winter of 1915-1916, the war escalated like a crescendo into a cruel struggle against the forces of nature and a dogged fight for the 3,344 metre-high summit, culminating in ever greater horrors.

The Marmolada watch

The well-known architect Fritz Malcher died in New York on 4th October 1933 aged 45 as a result of a routine appendix operation. With more luck he could obviously have aspired to higher things, but finished his life as a man who achieved much and left much incomplete. In New York he designed streets and squares, while in Vienna he submitted a plan to redesign the city's present-day main shopping street, the Kärntner-Strasse.

However his hands were tied by a lack of funds and obstructive bureaucracy, while in New York the Austrian from Baden near Vienna was prevented from tackling the design of an entire street because of problems with his work permit.

Fritz Malcher was called to the Dolomite front in autumn 1915 aged 27. His father, Rudolf, a South African merchant had sent him to study architecture in Vienna and Munich. His operational area was the front on the Marmolada. Life was fairly tranquil for him in 1915 and he first experienced the horrors of war at the beginning of 1916. However, before events escalated on the front he married Lotte

Buchler at Christmas in Trieste. His great passion was photography. Day by day he captured the events in detail with his large camera on glass lantern slides. They are moving, first-hand witnesses to life on the front line, to the optimism and the agony. Few others managed to document the First World War chronologically in pictorial sequences, day by day to provide such a forceful, comprehensive view. He remained on the Marmolada until the battles became more and more gory and murderous. He witnessed the first underground galleries and palaces within the glacier. Then one day Fritz Malcher fell and was badly injured. The active war ended for him but continued in his mind. He arranged his lantern slides and presented them to a small audience. Fritz Malcher, architect from Baden near Vienna held a lecture on his war experiences on the Marmolada front as a contemporary witness on 16th November, 1926. Extracts from his photographic diary were published for the first time.

Autumn 1915

Fritz Malcher recorded events and conditions exactly as they were day by day as if in a photographic diary. On his first day, together with many others he was billeted in the Karersee-Hotel, headquarters of the command for the Marmolada section of the front. Malcher still enthused over the "alluring beauty of the Rosengarten" mountain. "And the view back to the Karer pass with the Latemar massif rising behind is simply splendid." At the beginning of the war the entire area was defended by the 90th Infantry Division under the command of Lieutenant Field Marshal von Scholz-Bennoburg and the Bavarian Alpine Corps. In October 1915 the Bavarians were subsequently relieved after six months by the 4th Kaiser-jäger ('Emperor's Own') regiment. At that point things became bitterly serious for the future architect. They decamped, marching past the huts of the Russian prisoners of war workers. The Marmolada was a strategically-important summit which had to be occupied.

Above: By then snow had already settled on the Pordoi-Joch pass and soldiers had to push the car laboriously uphill. At the summit they were confronted for the first time with the awful realities of war. Above, right: The first fallen soldiers lie buried in a secluded graveyard. Apart from a number of patrols the Marmolada massif was for the most part still unaffected by the war, though this situation was soon to change radically. By the end of July 1915 the front had been pushed forward, eastwards to Arabba and bordered directly on to the Col di Lana peak which was to gain notoriety for all the wrong reasons.

While the Italian troops were concentrating in the Val Cordevole valley the Austrians advanced via the Val di Fassa, through the Val Contrin to the south of the Marmolada up to the Ombretta pass and to the Fedaia pass in the north. During the first war months of 1915 hardly anybody was much interested in the actual summits of the Marmolada. People were confident that the war would end quickly. Above: The Pizatsc emplacement at an elevation of 2,200 m above sea level is protected with a makeshift barbed wire entanglement. Above, right: At the time there were still few lookouts guarding against enemy advances. In the foreground the solitary Pizatsc position sentry sees the Col di Lana before him with the peaks of the Tofane far beyond in the background.

The march continued from the Fedaja emplacement into the actual Marmolada area. This sector could be observed by the enemy, therefore a passageway was constructed as far as the Bescul emplacement, almost a kilometre long, and covered as protection from enemy fire. Rails were even laid to facilitate transport.

As if glued to the rock face a gun emplacement was constructed on a ridge at 2,700 metres on the Mezodì-Kreuz. Lieutenant Ulrich manned the position with a small company and a single old, small artillery piece 500 m from the Italian positions. He had to fire both to the north and the south moving it backwards and forwards on wheels.

Enemy shells continued to strike. Even if they were fired from a small 15 cm gun they sent rocks and stones hurtling metres high. Communication trenches connecting the positions were laboriously blasted out of the rocks leaving deep scars in the landscape.

Then came the winter of 1915-16. Left: Here the Fedaja position still appears tranquil. In the telephone shelter news arrived from all parts. Right: However in the course of one night events changed dramatically. The shelter van- ished beneath two metres of fresh snow, though where snowdrifts had accumulated the depth reached four metres (twelve feet). And this was far from the worst snowstorm during the First World War.

Hundreds of Russian prisoners of war were assigned the arduous task of clearing the tracks and roads. A snow cave had to be excavated to reach the door to keep the occupants supplied with food. In spite of being five metres tall the shelter was completely buried beneath snow. The Fedaja position was completely entombed and soldiers often had to be pulled up by hand. Positions on both sides fell quiet for days while the troops were preoccupied with shovelling themselves free rather than making war.

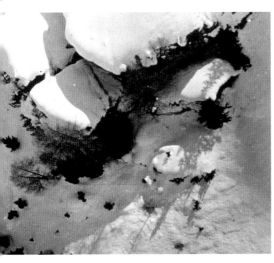

Several hastily improvised ropeway conveyors carried soldiers and equipment up to the mountaintop positions from Pian Trevisan bear Canazei.

Passenger transport was strictly forbidden though nobody paid much attention to the regulations. The high positions facing the Marmolada summit were reached by means of three cableways – the Gran Poz, the Col Bous and the D cable cars.

Below: The carriages soar 180 metres over a terrace in the rock-face. Higher up a strange occurrence took place which was luckily coupled with incredible fortune.

"Suddenly half way up the wire rope broke. A young cadet was sitting in the small carriage... The carriage with the cadet only fell as far as the increasing tension on the haulage rope would allow, then it flipped the carriage with the cadet high in the air – caused once again by tension in the cable – only to plummet anew. After being hurled up and down once more with a swing of around 40 m, on rising for the third time the young man lost consciousness and consequently his grip and flew headfirst in a wide arc into deep snow in a hollow 70 metres below. – He had vanished. – The men who had witnessed the awful spectacle at both terminals struggled to compose themselves after the shock, then began to climb down to the victim. Though not for long, for something moved suddenly below in the hole in the snow caused by the fall. A figure crawled out from the snow cussing and panting and very much alive. He had fractured his left collarbone, that was all." (Fritz Malcher – citations)

151

The sentry posts 1 to 5 are located in lofty positions at the foot of the glacier. An avalanche destroyed sentry post no. 3 which was rebuilt close by with a view of the Gran Vernel and the Mulon.

The barber ensures that the men are kept smart in appearance with the Langkofel massif behind. Above: In 1915 the highest position was at an altitude of 2,805 m. Here corn snow forms part of the emplacement's protection against enemy fire. The peaks of the Ombretta can be seen to the south-east. Such photographs were taken under extremely arduous conditions.

Steep mountainsides under deep snow cover in winter with a constant threat of avalanches were made practicable by constructing a covered step-way. This masterpiece of human ingenuity was called the 'Stairway to Heaven'. It connected the Pra di Contrin with the Col Ombert.

Over a hundred men were required day in day out whatever the weather for the sole purpose of supplying the units on the Costabella and Lastei-Scharte col. The backbreaking uphill climb was in full view of the enemy and thus continuously under fire.

A shelter was improvised there, close to the Lastei col. Tunnels in the snow connected the various positions.

A sensational photograph. On the Lastei col a solitary picket carries out his duty in a forward position at the end of a ladder which was wedged in the rock and led up through a cleft. (Arrow)

Nowhere was the enemy so close. The adversaries were only seven metres apart.

And so the by the end of 1915 the Austrians had managed to establish positions everywhere on the Marmolada, sometimes in places which were so exposed that to us today it seems unimaginable how they could have been manned day and night, both in summer and in winter without letting their guard down. This position on the Allochet ridge formed the southern limit of the Marmolada defences and certain sentinels must have led a hermit's existence in such conditions. Sometimes temperatures plummeted below minus 20 centigrade for weeks on end, blizzards and storms raged over the shelters while in summer the exposed positions amid bare rock were constantly struck by lightning. Who could not shudder at the thought of holding out and fighting under such conditions. Pictures such as these bring home to us the grim reality of the war.

Nevertheless soldiers still found moments for carefree merrymaking in spite of the conditions. Massive snowfall during the winter of 1915-16 brought the actual fighting to a halt. Men took advantage of the lull to consider how to better challenge the enemy and how to build safe supply routes to positions among the peaks.

1916

A wire ropeway conveyor was to be built from Canazei up to the Sella-Joch saddle with a connection to the Pordoi-Joch pass. Such cableways had proved to be the most practical means of transport. However constructing them involved enormous feats of strength. Hundreds of mainly Russian prisoners of war were deployed first of all to clear the road leading up to the Sella pass which was under metres of snow. They were then harnessed like beasts of burden to the enormous boiler and drive components of the electricity generator to haul the leviathan uphill. For many kilometres. It was mounted on sledge runners to keep the weight moving more easily and in addition the load was also attached to the traction engine of a 30.5 Mörser heavy mortar, though it proved far too weak. On the other side of the Sella pass the gigantic payload's progress had to be laboriously retarded down to Canazei. This sequence provides an impressive picture of this superhuman feat.

At the beginning of 1916 the wire-rope conveyor – a technological marvel for the time - was finally operational after arduous construction work. This aerial cableway connected Canazei with the Sella pass with a branch to the Pordoi saddle.

It provided a fast and efficient means of replenishing supplies unhampered by the enemy.

Men had little regard for their own safety. They invariably preferred a fast but uncomfortable and perilous ride to a long march and hazard the consequences.

The following scenes document the capture and securing of the Marmolada summit at over 3,300 metres above sea level. Until the end of 1915 this region had remained unscathed by the war events but soon the strategic importance of the 3,000 metre-high glacier became increasingly obvious, for its peaks dominated surrounding lower-lying areas. Consequently the Schölz-Hütte refuge was built in the Marmolada col (top picture picket dugout) beneath an overhanging mass of rock to withstand Italian attacks. It was named after General Scholz, commander of the 90th infantry division.

The *Scholz-Hütte* refuge situated on the western ridge of the Marmolada at an altitude of 3,042 provided accommodation for the 50 men assigned the task of holding the summit. They made the hut as cosy as possible. These unique pictures show the 'inauguration' of the Schölz refuge on Easter Sunday, 1916. Outside a hurricaneforce wind was blowing, overhanging masses of snow crashed down but still the atmosphere inside the hut is festive. But then they had had to carry up each plank and board in backbreaking corvee. The Austrian troops made history with this venturesome feat.

They continued developing and improving this forward position until the end of May 1916. An artillery piece was even hauled up and mounted on the northern ridge of the Marmolada.

In February and March 1916 material was carried up to reinforce and extend the summit position at an altitude of 3,344 metres. Pathways were dug into the slopes and the danger of avalanches was acute. In many cases they were only able to work at night or in fog. Bottom: In daytime soldiers had to wear white coats as camouflage when working in the open. Two soldiers patrol the area on the western ridge at an altitude of 3,100 metres.

"February, 10 degrees below zero. ... A large column of silent men trudges laboriously up across the glacier towards the Marmolada gap. Climbing in pairs carrying two-metre-long planks or lengths of squared timber, under the heavy weight some soldiers sink to their knees in fresh snow which had fallen during the day. ... The cold penetrates their mittens, slowly their hands become numb and they can no longer feel the grips. ... The blasts of the storm become more and more violent and they can only find relief by cowering in bowls in the compacted corn snow. ... Again the man in front climbs up the rock, secures himself and the man behind toils up with his plank on his back. He has hardly managed a few steps when a blast hits his plank and raises it. The soldier holds on to it for dear life. The storm catches the man and his plank and raises both. "Let go" shouts the leader who sees this dreadful moment from the rear in a sudden flash of moonlight. The man lets go, falls and the plank falls down the southern face to the Italians. ....

"The man in front helps as best he can with the rope and the men struggle up to the height of 3,166 m, where the weathervanes on the cap of corn snow blow across the ridge. From there it is easier. The nèvè is less and less broken by rock terraces, the column closes and after a further half hour – one and a half from the gap – they reach the summit. There the planks and lengths of squared timber are stacked and before long the process of building the hut can begin. After a short rest they begin the descent. ... Suddenly the clouds have vanished and the moon shines unhindered on the column. At that point there is nothing left to do but run, for bullets hiss and crackle over their heads. ....

"Like a fantastic firework display explosions and shrapnel rain down on the glacier bathed in moonlight, the sound of explosions is piercing and cause rumbling echoes form the ice and rock faces of the Marmolada." (Fritz Malcher's account)

The fight for the summit was won. The soldiers' quarters were built on the Punta Penia at an altitude of 3,344 m. Above all it was a victory for their own ego, just like the first ascent of a peak.

The shelter on the summit of the Marmolada was small, designed for six persons, built entirely in the ice and very quickly enclosed in it. For a long time the enemy did not harass the summit position, the main adversary were the elements which raged and tormented them incessantly – however breathtaking and romantic the view was from the summit.

"Six men sat together tightly in the small hut without reflecting on the danger as the thunderstorm gathered, darkening the sky. Small sparks flashed between the nails in their boots and crackled from one shoe to the other. It was uncanny. They quickly took off their shoes and threw everything containing metal: rifles, axes, picks, wire etc out of the door, even the small stove. They had hardly finished when there was a deafening bang and all six men were lying on the floor, flung down by the compensation of electrical tension which developed around the shelter, for it was not the metal objects which attracted the lightning but the ice surrounding the hut. Lightning struck seven times in succession, tormenting the men with its dreadful game. They crouched on the floor and were flung down again each time. Reeling and almost unconscious they were helpless against such force."
(Fritz Malcher)

The Italians could not simply shrug off the fact that the Austrians had occupied the strategically important highest summits of the Marmolada. In a surprise attack daring Italian soldiers belonging to the 'Cordevole' Alpini battalion took the Serauta arête on 8th April 1916. From then on the Serauta ridge at 2,900 metres and the Serauta summit a little higher at 3,035 metres overlooking the main glacier of the Marmolada were fought-over bitterly. During the exceptionally cold night of 13th April 1916 and under the most adverse circumstances the Austrian troops managed to recapture the Serauta ridge and hold on to it in spite of the awful environmental conditions. Until 30th April 1916, when the Italian troops retook the ridge once and for all under Captain Menotti Garibaldi, a relation of the famous freedom fighter. It was a victory with enormous symbolic power. 1,800 metres of hemp rope were used to conquer the ridge in a lightning attack.

Bitter conflicts raged around the Serauta summit throughout the summer of 1916. The Austrians became concerned about keeping the position supplied and began to consider creating connections between the single positions using the glacier crevasses and fissures. This was literally breaking new ground. At the time nobody had any experience of creating a permanent settlement in the bowels of a glacier. Thereafter the army began to build entire barracks in the glacial ice.

Fritz Malcher's superb photographic and documentary account of this part of the war in the Dolomites concludes with this picture. A new pioneer continued writing the war history. The spiritual father of the 'Ice City', young twenty-nine year-old Captain Leo Handl.

'City in the Ice'

The Serauta had to be held by the Austrians at all costs. This order was received by the twenty-nine year-old Captain Leo Handl via Major Bilgeri. And it went down in history because of an innovation: galleries in the glacial ice. He made out two crevasses on the edge of the glacier and wanted to connect them with the emplacement at the southern foot of the Zwölfer (Dodici).

He described the beginning of his task: "I immediately had work started in several places on the network of tunnels which I had designed on the map. Unfortunately the valuable explosives ran out rather quickly but we made up for that by employing ice axes, boring tools so efficiently that in 24 hours of continuous work we could advance 6 to 8 metres. It was all go in autumn 1916. Wooden huts were built in open crevasses at suitable points in the middle of the glacier, from where we tunnelled in two directions."

Together with the mountain guide Antonio Jori from Penia in the Val di Fassa Leo Handl continued to find new crevasses which made the tunnelling easier. In autumn 1916 there was already a gallery labyrinth over eight kilometres long beneath the Marmolada glacier.

The military chaplain Martin Matschik was very popular among the soldiers on the Marmolada. They esteemed him as an understanding padre though still more as a comrade and fellow traveller in the midst of those horrific times of war. When the knell sounded for a soldier he gave him comfort, murmured profound words of consolation and helped him as best he possibly could up there in the Marmolada glacier ice. In 1916 an intensive network of galleries and gangways, caves and fissures in the ice traversed this Dolomite glacier and the so-called 'City of Ice' assumed a

Andrea de Bernardin of the War Museum on the Fedaia pass on the Marmolada looks from a gallery out onto the sea of ice.

mystical appearance. The Kaiserschützen even built an 'Ice Church' for the chaplain for which he was forever grateful to them. Leo Handl was a great thinker and innovator. Hardly anywhere else had the Italians occupied a better strategic position than there and death mowed down row upon row of soldiers in such an awful, cruel way. That is until Leo Handl had the

A selection of pictures giving insight into the fascination of these man-made citadels in the glacial ice, often 40 metres below the surface. Glacier ice moves constantly and for this reason special attention needed to be given to secure bridges and underground constructions. Below: Several sunglasses used during the First World War are on show in the Mürzuschlag Ski Museum. Various materials were experimented with.

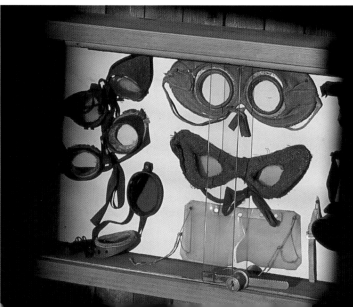

ingenious idea of burrowing gangways and galleries into the glacier. He had heavy-duty tools and boring equipment brought up, tried out numerous explosives in the ice but the technological difficulties soon became obvious: the poisonous gases generated by the explosives could not escape from the galleries, forcing Leo Handl to invent new methods though in most cases he finished up resorting to traditional, tried and tested manual means. Ice axes and thrust tools were procured and a host of soldiers began laboriously to tunnel through the mountain.

At last over 1,000 metres difference in elevation had been bridged safe in the bowels of the glacier. Up to an altitude of 3,259 metres. Previously soldiers had had to endure temperatures of below minus 30 and exposure to raging storms, while inside the glacier the temperature rarely dropped below zero. Soldiers were no longer terrorised to such an extent by dangers posed by snowstorms and avalanches, bullets and shells. Men were awestruck by the grandeur of nature: malachite-green walls

This atmospheric picture of a soldier taking a break outside one of the galleries hardly seems to emanate from the war.

alternated with blue, translucent seams of ice, glistening deep-blue crystals in their thousands gave way to gleaming, deep-blue icicle formations. It became a wartime fairytale castle with one lord: Graduate Engineer Leo Handl. Now win-dows in the southern face of the Marmolada provided views of the enemy positions which no longer had room for manoeuvre. The Italians did try to build an opposing tunnel of their own to blow up an important section and the Austrians came close

This impressive photo shows the military chaplain of the Kaiserschützen Regiment III Martin Matschik saying mass in an ice cavern. His commitment and readiness to help towards the soldiers is legendary. He celebrated mass deep within the bowels of the glacier.

meeting the same fate as their comrades on the Col di Lana, where the Italians succeeded in blowing up a gallery dug beneath the Austrian position. However, before they could bring their plan to fruition the Italians were ordered to abandon the Dolomite front in autumn 1917 after the German-Austro-Hungarian breakthrough at Caporetto (Karfreit).

Nevertheless the citadel deep in the glacier took an atrocious toll. The masses of ice pressed down on the tunnels with tremendous force, causing them and the glacier bridges to collapse. Soldiers lost their way among the endlessly long and extensive labyrinth of galleries. If the candlelight

went out inadvertently it became impossible to move and there was a great danger of falling over ledges. In addition many soldiers became ill from the constantly cold and damp climate in the ice galleries. They suffered from rheumatism, gout and pains in their joints. And in spite of everything there were countless dead on both sides. In 1916 Captain Rudolf Schmid gave the macabre order that corpses of fallen soldiers should not be buried in the ice and snow for fear of contaminating the drinking water. Where there was too little earth – and that was almost always the case – the bodies were to be carried down to the valley manually.

It is impressive how huge and intricately constructed these caverns and galleries were. Various sections were given sentimental names: 'The Dome', 'Kaiser Franz Josef Crevasse', and as memorials to Austria's capital city, 'Kärntner-Strasse' and 'St. Stephen's Cathedral'.

One of the most macabre pictures from the First World War in the Dolomites. The remains of an unfortunate Italian soldier emerge from the snow on Monte Piano in spring 1917. Only in death did adversaries become so close.

Avalanches, the impartial 'White Death'

Events as early as March 1916 provided a foretaste of what was to come when 280 Italian soldiers and 19 civilians were swept to their deaths in the Marmolada area. Above all the winters in the war years 1915-1917 were characterised by phenomenal volumes of snowfall of a kind hitherto unknown in human memory. Furthermore, units stationed high up in the regions of eternal ice desperately needed to be kept in supplies. The first weeks of December 1916 already saw the horrors of the war in the Dolomites enhanced when a third, more awful adversary joined the fray. It snowed almost incessantly for days on end until on the Fedaja pass it stood 12 metres high in places. In many secluded positions soldiers had to hold out without any prospect of receiving longed-for relief or supplies, while below in the valley men felt for their comrades fighting for the fatherland isolated among the peaks but knew that it was often hopeless to attempt an as-

cent and even where it would have been possible the danger of avalanches was far too acute. Still the powers of nature afforded little respite. At the beginning of December Rudolf Schmid, captain of the Marmolada battalion, requested from his superiors permission to abandon the encampment quickly. The massive falls of snow had "left so little room for manoeuvre that an enemy attack on many positions is improbable." The request was refused. By mid December some 50 Landesschützen dead had been claimed by avalanches.

Then on the 13th December 1916 a thaw set in accompanied by a strong, warm föhn wind which brought spring-like temperatures to the Alps. The priest Martin Matschik, legendary chaplain to the 1st battalion of the 3rd Kaiserschützen regiment on the Marmolada remembered: "On that morning at around 5.30 we heard a dull rumbling, followed by an eerie silence."

Above: Russian prisoners of war were victims of an avalanche on the Lagazuoi in March 1916. Left: Soldiers dig out an artillery piece buried under metres of snow by an avalanche in the Fischlein valley.

An avalanche had thundered down from Punta Rocca, one of the Marmolada summits, sweeping away the huts and barracks of the Grand Poz encampment in the Fedaja sector with the dreadful force of a quarter of a million tonnes of snow moving at 200 kilometres per hour. 230 Kaiserschützen troops along with a 103 man-strong Bosnian supply column lay buried beneath the masses of snow. Including Lieutenant Colonel Schmid, who it took seven hours to free from his icy prison.

The great avalanche disaster on the Marmolada

Lieutenant Colonel Viktor Scherf was one of the rescuers: "We uncovered dead and more dead, a great many of them were our glorious youth..." They only managed to save 45 men, 270 died beneath this avalanche. It claimed more dead than any other avalanche catastrophe on the Alpine front. Josef Strohmaier, one of the lucky survivors wrote: "We saw a confusion of beams, boards, arms, bodies and heads. In front a man danced and sang ghoulishly, for he had gone insane." This avalanche accident with its hundreds of casualties could easily have been avoided with a little less obstinacy and more intuitive understanding, like numerous others which occurred in those days, each of which claimed twenty or thirty dead. Viktor Scherf was devastated and reported: "But there was one thing they brought in masses: coffins, repeatedly. It was the first time in the battle zone and on the front that we received too much of something." More than four days after the avalanche five freezing, pale figures crawled out from their cold grave looking like ghosts. Working day and night they burrowed their way through six metres of snow driven by their will to survive and in this way escaped death. Unfortunately an order had been given – obviously not by an officer who knew the Alps – to save space in the huts by storing all tools, shovels and picks outside. Of course they were swept away by the avalanche, a mistake which cost numerous lives for the soldiers were left with

The Austrian barracks below the Gran Poz summit, shown here before the devastating avalanche, had been improved in spring 1916. The encampment served to supply summit positions on the Marmolada.

nothing but their bare hands to burrow with. On the positive side this avalanche disaster increased knowledge and awareness of the peril. Hitherto it was considered almost impossible for anybody to survive for days under an avalanche even under the most favourable conditions.

According to official figures issued by the Austrian high command alone in these two days 6,000 soldiers perished beneath avalanches. How many Italians met the same fate, and how many casualties went unreported? We will never know. The task of determining how many men lost their lives on the mountains is extremely difficult. Bodies were will being uncovered in early summer. Those who were buried alive had often scraped their fingers to the bone as they fought to dig themselves free in their struggle against suffocation. Time

and again even the glacier galleries and underground tunnels on the Marmolada were engulfed by enormous masses of snow and threatened the occupants with suffocation. Many dug themselves out of the masses of ice in a desperate race against time, though for many others there came no rescue. Even today the icy grave continues to yield up the remains of its victims. Hardly ever before had nature played such a decisive role in war. Only one third of the men who died fighting in this bloody war in the mountains were actually killed in action. The other two thirds fell victim to avalanches and lightning, landslides and rock falls. In three years 60,000 men were killed alone by the awesome destructive power of avalanches. Tragedies and individual fates evoke scenes of horror and devastation.

Russian prisoners of war at work digging the barracks free from the metres-high snow masses. The avalanche claimed almost three hundred lives.

The avalanche disaster in the Landro valley

One of the worst avalanche disasters of the war occurred near Schluderbach on 28th February, 1916, killing over 260 men. Initially 20 soldiers forming part of an advance troop had marched to the Gemärk saddle close to the Raukofel and were struck by an avalanche. There followed a scene of unimaginable horror when troops in the rear rushed forward to help. At that moment an even larger mass of snow broke free from the slopes of the Raukofel and engulfed the entire two companies. For a time this entire sector of the front lay undefended. This event revealed the sense of honour which still prevailed among the warring parties, for the Italians made no attempt to take advantage of the Austrians' distress and fired not a single shot to dis-

rupt the rescue operations. By daybreak most of the soldiers had been dug out, a large number of which were badly disfigured.

The 'White Death' had claimed the lives of more than 250 common soldiers and NCOs, 6 officers and one military chaplain. Many Italians had to accustom themselves to the harsh winters with deep snow in the high mountains. In a great rush stoves, metal sleds, packaging materials, blankets, skis and everything imaginable required for a tough winter war had to be procured. Forests were cut down to provide essential fuel. Hastily improvised wooden barracks became death traps, smoke escaped too slowly through the chimneys and choked the men. Vast numbers suffered from frostbite. Rifles froze to solders' fingers causing painful and lasting open wounds.

Sulla strada da Greppe a Prà Pontin

Left: An Italian Alpino soldier has dug a tunnel to his hut lying beneath several metres of snow. Right: The snow towers like cliffs on each side of the road from Greppa to Prà Pontin. The route had to be laboriously shovelled clear.

Although fighting was scaled down in winter attacks never ceased completely, for both sides hoped that perhaps during the cold season they could manage to gain important tactical advantages to surprise the enemy. New materials were introduced which had never been tried and tested but nevertheless supplied to the troops in their thousands. There were shoes made of pasteboard which, according to the suppliers were much better than the traditional leather boots. Unfortunately they were not pliable, impaired blood circulation, while snow penetrated into the insole leading to frostbite. Winter greatcoats were often not issued to individuals but to entire companies. Clothing also had to be altered. Both Austrians and Italians put on white outer clothing as camouflage to render themselves inconspicuous in the white landscape. Pack animals were shod with special high horseshoes.

Fortunately by the time the second winter of the war came round lessons had been learnt to avoid the disasters encountered the year before. Roofs were reinforced and where possible caverns and dugouts were excavated in the rock. Signs warning of 'Avalanche Danger' were put up, while skiers and supply bearers were given so-called 'avalanche strings' to enable rescue parties to find them and dig them out more quickly. Each winter patrol faced incalculable risks. Telegraphy was often the only means of communicating with snow-bound units holding out high up in the mountains.

During the winter of 1917 snow accumulated reaching depths unknown in living memory. Tunnels were dug in the snow in order to avoid avalanche casualties and even to keep supply lines open. They were often of considerable length and height.

One of the most disastrous avalanche catastrophes of the entire war took place on 28th February 1916 sweeping over 260 soldiers to their deaths.

Tiroler Kaiserjägermuseum - Berg Isel - Innsbruck

We have to put the slaughter behind us

Giacomo Alberti

June 1924: on the western slopes of the Tofàna de Rozès, Serafino Siorpaes de Valbòna (right) of Cortina and a colleague from Val Badia recover the remains of a dead soldier. Above left there are remains of Italian ammunition. Life and death are portrayed here gruesomely side by side. The mortal remains of this unfortunate person are meagre compensation for his successors. It is not appropriate here to speak of morals – the naked will to survive triumphed.

Istituto Culturale Ladin, Vigo

The painter Franzeletto Bernard painting a grave cross in the military cemetery Santa Giuliana in the Val di Fassa.

Peace reigns once again

For the Italians the war ended at 3pm on 4th November 1918, for the Austrians at midnight on 3rd November. One of many similar misunderstandings. It ended in a vale of tears and destruction on all sides. The burden of this 'Great War', as it soon became reverently known, changed this mountain region and the scars remain to this day. An odd feeling of insecurity prevailed.

Was one a loser for having fought on the side of the defeated nation? Was a new injustice committed? Thoughts of victory and defeat were suppressed and the 'Great War' was consigned, to history. People appraised their situation but still were brought down to earth by reality. The victors and the defeated had to learn to live with the changes. Italy was given Trentino and parts of Friuli including the city of Trieste, territories which were mainly Italian-speaking. However, she was also granted South Tyrol with its German and Ladin-speaking population.

In the end the means of sustaining life were largely lacking. There was no daily bread. As the war progressed soldiers had to make do with half a tin of meat, instead of fresh vegetables they had a little dried fruit and swede, a vegetable which before the war was only fed to animals. Bread was stretched with ground corncob, tree bark and potatoes. The average soldier weighed just 55 kg (under 9 stone), 75 percent of children were undernourished. Coffee was made from caramelised sugar, turnip flour and a little real coffee; on the front it was brewed over and over until the final prod-

Winter 1916 at Canazei in the Val di Fassa. The first signs of food shortages become noticeable. Kaiserjäger soldiers of the 4th Regiment serve up soup to the starving populace. Right: children collecting rags at Sand in Taufers.

Günther Obwegs, Gottfried Lettgeb

uct resembled a light soup. Fat was extracted from animal carcasses and bones – they even tried to recover fat from washing-up water.

A new insidious death lowered, a devastating flu epidemic of hitherto unknown magnitude. It came at the end of the war unexpectedly and unidentified, spreading from Spain to the whole of Europe. In Switzerland it was thought to be the plague, while Austrian attack forces initially thought that the sick Italians languishing in the trenches were suffering from the effects of poison gas. It spread around the globe, causing some twenty million deaths.

Finally a start was made on collecting the unknown dead from the battlefields, on rebuilding villages and repairing the destruction in general. And on forgetting. 689,000 Italians died, on the Austro-Hungarian side the figure was 922,000 dead, further 855,283 "missing presumed dead". The two sides suffered nine million wounded, crippled and prisoners of war.

The war may have finished, but not the tribulations. National borders were shifted backwards and forwards. Nobody was satisfied. Italy had expected more, the Austrian Empire was shattered. The parties began to lick their wounds and clean up what the war had left behind. Bombs and mines lay around in the combat areas along with masses of iron, while year after year the receding snow yielded up the remains of unknown soldiers. Or they lay in inaccessible gullies.

'Recuperanti' or 'recuperators' was the name given to those who immediately set about clearing the mountains of the vestiges of the war. Initially there was very little to eat in the Dolomite villages and few means of earning money. Money was paid for iron shrapnel fragments, also for barbed wire collected in the mountains, laboriously collected and carried down to the valley. There was the constant danger of unexploded shells and grenades going off. Soon tourists began to return to the mountains, initially former combatants.

The Kaiserjäger soldier Angelo Ellecosta from Enneberg at the grave of his brother, Josef, who fell in Russia. A young Standschütze praying for the first comrades who fell in the war.

Enemies become friends

This mountain war was fought along a line of almost four hundred kilometres. It ate itself into the landscape like rampant festering sores. Immediately after the war people did all they could to remove traces of the war. The war wounded and killed. The war broke old friendships and destroyed human values.

The wounds proved not to be indelible. Gradually people began to reflect on revaluing this collective remembrance as part of our history by erecting memorials, marking peace pathways, equipping museums and setting out other places of commemoration.

Many man-made caverns which had collapsed were repaired as if people were determined to prevent these 'dead eyes' from sinking into oblivion. People from various nations, in many cases former enemies, worked together to restore barracks, trenches and galleries for the benefit of later generations. They breathed new life into them. Countless people began to collect whatever they could to document this world war: letters and diaries, photos, weapons, works of art. Interest in the war has never been stronger.

Interested persons can revisit the former battlefields today and experience them with other eyes. Relics of this ferocious struggle, man against man though above all, man against nature, can be found everywhere in these mountains. Numerous people have dedicated themselves to the cause with the intention of spreading tidings of peace through museums, building up documentation centres.

Whether they founded museums, preserved original settings and landscapes, or even maintained cemeteries, they are all deserving of thanks. Future wars can only be avoided if the ones which have gone before can be understood and digested.

179

The unknown martyr

There are occasional monumental chance discoveries in life. The Roman architect Fabio Ortolani was sauntering through a flea market in Rome when he stumbled on an inordinately large photo album measuring 74 x 51 cm.

Its contents sent shivers down his spine. It turned out to be a unique historical document, a memorial and warning for future generation. Essentially the album consisted of almost one hundred photos with a laboriously hand-coloured introductory page. The spine-chilling history which it narrates is quickly summarised: it documents the exploratory tour by the Italian 'mortuary police' in the valley of Cortina d'Ampezzo which took place over twenty days, from 19th September to 10th October 1920, when a sudden snow storm put an end to the sorry operation, as if pre-ordained by fortune. Dubbed the 'death police', they were given the task of exhuming the corpses buried in the cemeteries scattered throughout the mountains and valleys and to rebury them in a single place.

They were ordered to find and recover even the forgotten skeletons in shelters and dugouts throughout the wilderness, of soldiers who had fallen into the most inaccessible ravines and gullies. The 'Committee for the Honour of the World War Dead' in Trento was appointed with the macabre task. A photographer was specially assigned to the party who, aware of the unhappy importance of his work, took distressing photos one after the other. He carried out his work in a matter-of-fact manner like a reporter. The album itself became an unparalleled document of death.

For the fine, clear lines written in white ink lead directly into the depths of a world of awe and horror. The Ampezzo bowl is closed to the north, its boundaries marked by the ridge formed by the cyclopean massifs, from Lagazuoi to Tofane, from Valon Bianco to Croda d'Ancona, to Cristallo. The valley and the surrounding mountains were the scene of the most awful bloodshed.

Around 6,000 young men died here, their remains buried in 48 cemeteries. The task in 1920 was to collect them all and rebury them in a single cemetery at Cortina d'Ampezzo. The 'death police' went about their work meticulously. Their intention was to inform family relatives of the fallen as to where they found the skeletons, which methods were used to exhume the bodies and of the enormous efforts they put into retrieving them. However, they failed to realise how they themselves contributed to the death cult, for the images shown constituted a hitherto unimaginable and macabre dance of death.

In the photo human bones are stacked to form a mountain, dozens and dozens of skulls lie on the ground and it looks as if the sextons had their work cut out to prevent them from rolling down the steep slope. As they took their leave it seems as if they were asking for a final applause from us late-comers for their work they carried out, fully aware of their own self-sacrifice. Empty graves can be seen amid deep snow drifts. The very last unknown soldiers are buried here. Was it an Austrian, someone from the Ladin valleys, an Italian? Or perhaps somebody from a distant country? We are unlikely ever to find out.

Human remains are unearthed everywhere, in the woods and rocky gullies, and must be laboriously recovered.

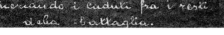

Arch. Fabio Ortolani

Pictures such as these two are accompanied by words in white ink such as "The fallen are fished out from among the vestiges of the battle"; and "Soldiers' remains found between crumbling rocks are brought to the place of burial".

"Flowers grow meekly from an amorphous pile of bones." A multitude of bones are stacked neatly. Alone the pithy sentences are an art form of their own.

"To the unknown martyr" is the caption written neatly by the author of the photo album to accompany this dramatic picture. Three years after the end of hostilities the fallen soldier has hardly begun to decompose.

Padre Domenico De Rocco from Forno di Canale (present-day Canale d'Agordo) in the Belluno Dolomites administers the last rites to the dead.

"Human skulls amid the scree where once battle raged." A policeman deep in thought seems no longer up to his assignment.

Maurizio Vicenzi, Peio (4)

The last days of humanity

In August 2004 the mummified corpses of three Austrian Kaiserschützen soldiers were discovered by the mountain guide Maurizio Vicenzi from Peio, yielded up by a glacier at 3,640 metres altitude in the Ortler-Cevedale massif. How can the death and barbarity of this war be explained to later generations?

Certainly not by a blunt presentation of the facts. Nothing should be concealed. A human life counted for little in this First World War, the mother of all even crueller conflicts of the 20th century. Death came in various ways, by bullet and shrapnel, though also through the rigours of nature, exposure, disease, hunger and privation. Or by hanging, firing squad or being shot in the back for hesitating in the face of enemy fire. How can the war be documented and presented in a way which ensures that others are avoided? A question which is often asked. For the essential nature of a war is not revealed in heroic actions glorified in the print and other media, but it is rather above all the unplumbed depths of human drives and avarice, suffering and revulsion which should be emphasised to document war. This is eminently achieved in these pictures.

The exact place where the three Austrian soldiers were found, exposed after almost a century by the receding glacier. They were recovered in order to bury them in the valley. Their torn clothing fluttered in the wind. They were not carrying weapons, just a gasmask and a water bottle. Probably their comrades took the other useful objects, for they were of no further use to these soldiers while for the survivors they may have been life-saving. There were few nails left in their boots, hardly suitable for this terrain. One soldier had no head, probably it was shot off. In death they were huddled together, as if they could keep each other warm and speak words of comfort to each other. Would it not have been better to leave them to rest in their icy grave?

Maurizio Vicenzi, Peio (4)

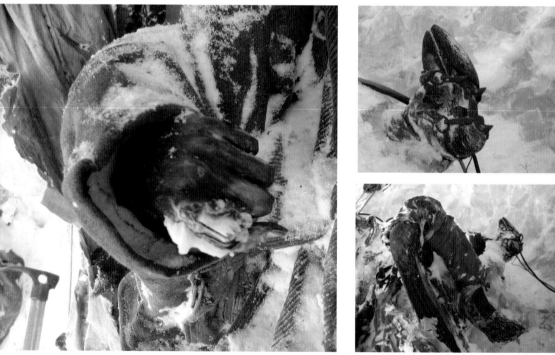

This is how the tattered remains of the three Austrian soldiers were found by the mountain guide and co-founder of the War Museum of Peio, Maurizio Vicenzi. Each individual picture recounts life and death. The three Kaiserjäger probably died this place. They were very young men on re-supply duties. As was the custom in these high regions, their comrades buried them in a crevasse.

186

Maurizio Vicenzi, Peio (4)

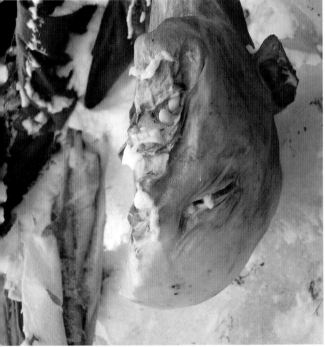

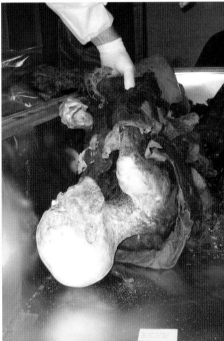

The blood-soaked hand is clenched, (left side) the face of the dead man contorted as in agony like the man in Edvard Munch's picture 'Scream'. Dentures replace teeth which had been lost prematurely, therefore he must have come from a fairly wealthy family. Maurizio Vicenzi is at the top (with a helmet recovering the corpses). One soldier was examined in the archaeological museum in Bolzano, the world centre for mummified bodies preserved in glacier ice.

Museo della Guerra Bianca, Temù - John Cerati

An Austrian gun, 10.4 cm, a 1915 model, which was yielded up by the glacier on the Adamello at an altitude of 3,171 m and recovered on 13th August 2003.

Coming to terms with one's destiny

We can only really come to terms with this war, which took place almost a century ago, when we are able to understand it objectively, free from any kind of nationalistic feelings. As long as we remain conditioned by our national allegiances we will stay prisoners of our own clichés and prejudices. Writers and film producers seized hold of the events and began to reappraise them from their own perspective before the war had finished.

The German author Erich Maria Remarque sold over a million copies of his book 'Nothing new in the west', while the British author Robert Graves achieved similar success with his 'Goodbye to all that', not to mention Ernest Hemingway's 'A Farewell to Arms' for which he won a Nobel Prize. The Italians Pietro Jahier and Emilio Lussu also wrote about the war. Curzio Malaparte served in the Dolomites during the war and wrote novels about his experiences, while Luis Trenker, initially Austrian, later 'Italian Tyrolean' or South Tyrolean after Austria lost his home valley to Italy, fought on the Lagauoi. His book 'Berge in Flamme' ('Mountains on Fire') was made into a successful film, as was the T. E. Lawrence 'of Arabia' book 'The Seven Pillars of Wisdom'. They all appealed to contemporary taste. Anton Bossi-Fedrigotti's novel 'Standschütze Bruggler' was turned into a film and apparently much admired by Adolf Hitler. This was a war which exceeded everybody's powers of imagination.

As the war progressed the tactics of all nations were no longer based on long-term strategic plans but on ad hoc measures, decisions taken simply to be seen to be doing something. One of the reasons was that the terrific toll on human life reached such magnitude that nobody could see a way out. Who would ever have imagined that a quarter of all British soldiers would die 'face-down in the mud'? Or that in the Alps a similar percentage of combatants would fall prey to avalanches? The latter were not killed by enemy fire. At the outset of hostilities who would have thought that so many fatalities would be due to poison gas?

When an entire company of Kaiser-schützen climbed the summit of the Marmolada during the winter of 1913 before the war there was an outcry because so many soldiers suffered from frostbite to their toes. This failed to send a message to the high command to provide better protective clothing. From the very beginning nobody was even interested in learning from past mistakes. During the war years the highest summits were occupied both in summer and winter with soldiers having to make do with insufficient materials, supplies and bad protective clothing. Lessons were finally learnt, but only after thousands of deaths.

One of the spin-offs from this war in the mountains was the rapid development of modern alpinism. By 1900 the Alps were attracting a handful of skiers, then during the war skis became important means of locomotion in the mountains. New skiing techniques were invented, of controlling speed by making turns and it is hardly surprising that the advice of former ski pioneers such as Bilgeri and Zdarsky was sought during the war.

It is superfluous to discuss death in war. It was at its cruellest when it struck in a soldier's most intimate circle. A soldier who lost his best friend or close comrade carried the memory with him for the rest of his life. The commander reported the name of the dead man to his superiors and finally he became part of the statistics: 347 dead, 222 missing in action. The same thing went for the wounded. A na-

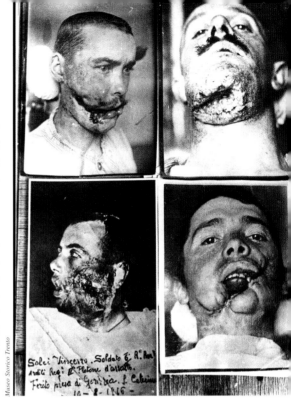

Museo Storico Trento

Above all, facial injuries resulted in awful deformations. Thanks to the enormous progress in medicine a soldier's life could be saved but the constant care and attention he required became a burden on his family. Constant exposure to bombardment and gunfire reduced men to so-called 'Kriegszitterer' or 'war tremblers', a condition which is now referred to as shell shock. The picture shows horribly disfigured Italian soldiers.

tional government had to be efficient enough to show strength even in wartime.

We do not and should not want to suppress from our minds the horrors of war. We need to come to terms with it continuously in constantly new variations. The picture of war should always shock and it is not the purpose of these pictures to soothe or play down its reality. There is no such thing as a war of heroes, that is a myth, there have only been wars of the dead.

The First World War in the Alps

1915

January - May

Italy initially declared herself neutral. The government soon began to waver, with both Austria-Hungary and the Allies competing for Italy's favour. A source of contention before the war had been the existence of several hundred thousand ethnic Italians living inside the Austrian Empire in territories which Italy claimed for herself. Britain, Russia and France tipped the balance by declaring their willingness to concede to Italy's demands.

23rd May

Italy declared war on Austria-Hungary and the first troops crossed the Piave river with the intention of breaking through a 600 km long front extending from the Swiss border to Slovenia, from the Adamello to the Dolomites, the Carnic and Julian Alps.

23rd June – 7th July

The insufficiently equipped Italian army became bogged down after the first battle against Austrian troops who had been hurriedly sent to defend the Empire's southern border. Above all the local Austrian volunteer units took up defensive positions among the rocks on all the major peaks and passes.

18th July – 3rd August

Although it had the effect of diminishing pressure on the Allies on the eastern front, the second battle fought under General Cadorna failed to produce the hoped-for Italian breakthrough.

18th October – 4th November

The third Isonzo battle ended in a fiasco like the preceding attacks. In the first year of the war the Italian army lost 300,000 men.

10th November – 2nd December

Likewise, the fourth Isonzo battle failed. In the mountains the Austrians had turned their positions into impregnable fortresses, making a breakthrough to the north almost impossible. The high mountain war began and both sides began adopting unprecedented tactics.

1916

11th – 16th March

The Italians attacked once again with the aim of taking Gorizia and the plateau of Doberdò. Once again it failed.

1st - 17th April

Fierce battles on Monte Cristallo. Italian Alpini troops occupied the Punta Serauta on the Marmolada as well as the Sentinella gap in the Sexten Dolomites. The Col di Lana summit was blown up by the Italians.

May

Austria began its so-called 'Strafexpedition' or 'punitive expedition' with the aim of advancing from South Tyrol through the Valsugana valley as far as Vicenza, but it eventually ground to a halt because of events elsewhere.

12th July

Cesare Battisti from Trento, an Austrian member of parliament and one of the symbolic figures of the Italian Irredentist movement, was captured fighting as an Italian officer and executed as a traitor.

8th August

In the sixth Isonzo battle the Italians took Gorizia but failed to advance on to Trieste.

September

The positions in the mountains were drastically improved and further fortified, especially those on the Ortler, the Adamello and the Marmolada in preparation for the second winter of the war. In spite of continuous heavy fighting neither side made significant gains.

November

The early onset of winter brought up to six metres of snow and halted hostilities. It was the worst winter in living memory and frequent avalanches took a terrible toll on human life on both sides.

1917

January

The enormous masses of snow in the mountains had brought to hostilities almost to a complete halt. Innovative tactics had produced promising results, such as the Austrian tunnels in the glacier ice on the Marmolada.

20th – 21st June

Italians exploded a mine under the Austrian position on the Lagazuoi. They took the summit but were unable to gain significant advantages.

18th August – 13th September

The eleventh Isonzo battle was the most bloody of all, but resulted in minimal territorial gains. Total Italian losses during the war amounted to almost 700,000, while the Austrians lost 430,000 men on this front (during the whole war 922,000 dead, further 855,283 missing "presumed dead"). War fatigue set in among the Italian troops. Cadorna reacted with firing squads and drumhead courts-martial.

24th October

Austrian-German formations attacked Italian troops at Plezzo and Tolmino. The unexpected breakthrough came at Caporetto (Kobarid in Slovenian, Karfreit in German): the Austrians captured 300,000 Italians, a further 400,000 civilians became refugees. The Austrian army penetrated deep into Italian territory and only halted at the Piave river. General Cadorna was dismissed and replaced with Armando Diaz. Italy was seething. In Austria people spoke of the wonder of Caporetto.

1st – 10th November

Following the successful German-Austrian offensive on the Isonzo river the Italians were forced to abandon their positions in the Dolomites and retreat. There was stalemate once again along the front on Monte Grappa and on the Pasubio. The Italian army needed to be built up once again and reorganised.

1918

15th – 22nd June

Under Field Marshals Conrad von Hoetzendorff and Boroevic von Bojna ('the Lion of the Insonzo') the Austrians crossed the Piave river in several places but were swiftly forced back.

15th June – 19th July 1918

Monte Cavento in the Adamello massif was recaptured by the Austrians a year after the Italians had taken it. It was taken back by the Italians on 19th July. Battles on the Ortler and the Adamello became increasingly fiercer after the withdrawal of the Russians on the eastern front.

23rd June

The Italians achieved a first victory. The Austrians lost 150,000 men, the Italians 90,000.

24th October

The Italians prepared for a large-scale attack with the support of the Allies. The Austro-Hungarian soldiers had difficulty resisting and were ordered to retreat to their original national borders. The Central Powers Austria and Germany were at the end of their tether, both militarily and politically.

3rd November

An armistice was signed between Austria-Hungary and Italy. Misconceptions arose as to the start of the ceasefire. Italian troops entered Trento and Trieste, taking thousands of prisoners. The Austrian army tried to escape home.

4th November, 3 p.m.

The war between Austria and Italy finally ended. South Tyrol became a predominantly German-speaking region of Italy.

An illusory peace was restored, the seed for the next war was sown.

'Peace upon earth!' was said. We sing it,

And pay a million priests to bring it.

After two thousand years of mass

We've got as far as poison gas.

Thomas Hardy, novelist and poet, 1840 – 1928

Arch. Fabio Ortolani

To the unknown soldier,

who was ordered,

to go to war against an enemy,

who he did not even know.